WHAT CRUCIFIED JESUS?

WHAT CRUCIFIED JESUS?

Messianism, Pharisaism, and the Development of Christianity

ELLIS RIVKIN

Foreword by Eugene J. Fisher

UAHC PRESS ♦ NEW YORK

Library of Congress Cataloging-in-Publication Data

Rivkin, Ellis, 1918–
What crucified Jesus? : messianism, pharisaism, and the development of Christianity / Ellis Rivkin ; foreword by Eugene J. Fisher.
p. cm.
Originally published: Nashville : Abingdon Press, 1984.
Includes bibliographical references.
ISBN 0-8074-0630-9 (pbk. : alk. paper)
1. Jesus Christ—Passion—Role of Romans. 2. Jews—History—168 B.C.–135 A.D. 3. Rome—Politics and government—30 B.C.–68 A.D. 4. Jesus Christ—Jewish interpretations.
BT431.6.R58 1997
232.96—dc21 97–11698
CIP

This book is printed on acid-free paper.

Manufactured in the United States of America

10 9 8 7 6 5 4 3 2 1

CONTENTS

FOREWORD

The reissuance of Ellis Rivkin's classic study is a cause for celebration among all those involved in the contemporary dialogue between Jews and Christians. And to have it augmented by five other essays, four published here for the first time, is an extraordinary gift to us all. Being asked to contribute a foreword provides me with the opportunity to express in a small way the gratitude my generation of Catholic scholars feels toward a generation of Jewish scholarship that came before us. When the Second Vatican Council in 1965 called on the Church to begin a fundamental reevaluation, a *cheshbon hanefesh*, of its teachings on Jews and Judaism, Rivkin and his colleagues around the world, such as David Flusser, Pinchas Lapide, Samuel Sandmel, and Geza Vermes, were already hard at work reading anew the New Testament with Jewish eyes.

This application of Jewish tradition and sensitivities to the New Testament has yielded a remarkable harvest of new insights into and perspectives on texts which, after all, were written in the main by Jews before the "parting of the ways" between Judaism and Christianity. Re-visioned through Jewish eyes, the New Testament comes alive in a way that could not have been anticipated by gentile Christians, even those few with some solid academic training in Jewish studies. We Catholics, who have worked to implement the Council's mandate to rethink the fundamental understanding of the relationship between Jesus and his people, God's people, the Jews, owe a great debt to the Jewish scholars who have taught us so much about our own sacred texts.

What Crucified Jesus? is one such text. Drawing on the ancient writings of Josephus and the scholarship of his own teacher Solomon Zeitlin, of blessed memory, Rivkin recounts the narrative of Jesus' life, ministry, and murder at the order of the Roman occupiers of his native land within the setting of its time and place in the first half of the first century of the common era. Having an understanding of the larger historical movements and political concerns of the primary actors of Jesus' life and times not only increases the drama of the narrative but our understanding of why key actors in the drama reacted as they did to Jesus and his message.

The five additional papers draw on a variety of sources, rabbinic as well as historical, to expound aspects of the texts and of Jewish tradition vital to a full understanding of the New Testament and the Jesus story. Each complements the others in bringing out a new facet for our consideration of such matters as the concept of Messiah that the New Testament authors were likely to have held as Jews when contemplating the Christ event, the Law as Paul, with his background in Pharisaism, would have understood it, and the political dimensions behind the arrest and execution of John the Baptist.

This is a rich feast indeed. It can be appreciated not just by scholars, who will be grateful to have these essays collected and at hand, but equally by educated nonspecialists. The volume will be of interest, too, to Jews no less than Christians. Rivkin clears up numerous misunderstandings of the New Testament texts that not only we Christians have long held but also some in the Jewish community hold. This dynamic of mutual clarification renders the book an ideal tool for use in dialogue groups, as well as in more formal educational settings. Rivkin manages to disabuse us of our misunderstandings and lead us into uncomfortable topics such as Anti-Semitism in the New Testament in a spirited yet irenic fashion that is itself a model of dialogical discourse.

Eugene J. Fisher
Associate Director
Secretariat for Ecumenical and
Interreligious Affairs
National Conference of Catholic Bishops

I

WHAT CRUCIFIED JESUS?

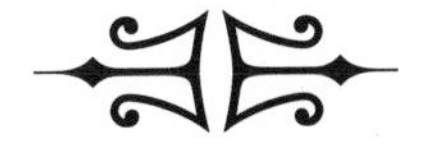

WHO CRUCIFIED JESUS?

It is tragic indeed that the birth pangs of Christianity were occasioned by an event in which Jews were directly implicated. It is tragic because it spawned intense hostility between mother and daughter religions, religions bound by an umbilical cord that can never be severed. As long as the Gospels, Acts, the Epistles of Paul, and the other books of the New Testament are read as Holy Scriptures by Christians, the tie to Judaism is a tie that binds. All Christian claims for Christ are grounded in verses from the Old Testament; all Christian claims to be the true Israel are underwritten by proof-texts drawn from the Pentateuch; and all Christian claims that Jesus had risen from the dead are embedded in the core belief of the Scribes-Pharisees of Jesus' day. Cut the history and the religion of Israel out of the New Testament and Christianity vanishes. The Old Testament may be replaced by the New, the Israel of the flesh by the Israel of the Spirit, and the Law by Christ, but the umbilical cord remains.

The umbilical cord remains, yet that tie has been taut with tragedy. Jesus died no ordinary death in no ordinary circumstances. According to the Gospels, he was arrested by order of the high priest; he was tried before a sanhedrin of Jewish notables presided over by the high priest; he was delivered over to the Roman procurator[1] by the high priest; he was condemned to crucifixion on the charge of claiming to be the King of the Jews; and he was resur-

[1]Although there is evidence that *procurator* was applied to Roman military governors only from the time of Claudius and therefore Pilate actually was called *prefect* of Judea, I prefer to retain the use of the familiar term, since substantively they are synonymous.

rected by God the Father three days after he had breathed his last. Throughout this horrendous process, Jews are in the forefront: the high priest, scribes, and elders; the sanhedrin; the hostile crowd calling for crucifixion; the Jews mocking his royal claim as Jesus hung on the cross twisted and dying. How, on hearing or reading this painful and shocking account of a teacher who has healed the sick, commiserated with the poor, exorcised demons, sat with sinners, and preached of God's coming kingdom, can one respond without pain, sorrow, and bitter anger? And Christians throughout the centuries have responded with pain, with sorrow, and with bitter anger against Jews, who seem to have caused it all.

Crucifixion was a cruel and inhumane act. It would have been cruel and inhumane even were the crucified one guilty of some serious crime. It plumbed the depths of cruelty and inhumanity when it was inflicted on a charismatic, a prophetic visionary, an earnest seeker of salvation and redemption for his people. Those who were ultimately responsible for so heinous a crime are deserving of our righteous wrath, if not of our righteous vengeance.

It is therefore understandable that the disciples of Jesus who witnessed his travail were shocked, outraged, embittered, and unforgiving of those whom they believed to have been responsible. It is also understandable that in the record of Jesus' life, trial, crucifixion, and attested resurrection, there should be so much violent hatred for all those who, in one way or another, had rejected him as the Messiah while he was alive and had rejected him as the Messiah after his disciples had seen him risen from the dead. Were the record otherwise, it would have to have been set down by angels, not beings of flesh and blood.

We cannot therefore shake off this frightening question of responsibility. The New Testament, like the Old, will always be with us. The story will always arouse pain, sorrow, and anger in the hearts of Christians. No surgical procedure can cut away the guts of the gospel story: an arrest, a trial, a crucifixion, and an attestation to a resurrection.

Nor should we dodge the question of responsibility. As seekers of truth, we would wish to know what occurred, why it occurred, and who was responsible for its occurrence. As seekers of reconciliation between the mother and the daughter religions, we would wish to build this reconciliation on the facing of facts rather than on the dissolving of them.

This twofold goal may perhaps be achieved if we shift our focus from the question *Who* crucified Jesus? to the question *What* crucified Jesus?

But that shifting of focus is more easily suggested than done. For we need some source for Jesus' life that is free of the hostile intensity of the gospel story—a source that would provide us with the historical Jesus, free of the passionate involvement of those who were certain that he had risen from the dead.

But where shall we find such a source? We have only the gospel record, a record penned with faith, written with passion, and bristling with hostility and resentment. So where are we to turn?

I suggest that we turn to the writings of Josephus—not because he records the life, the trial, the crucifixion, and the resurrection but because he does not! Josephus was born shortly after Jesus died and was a keen participant in and observer of the tumult of the time. As the general in charge of Galilee during the Jews' revolt against Rome, he was actively involved; and he wrote at great length of the road to war, first in *The Jewish War*, then in the last volumes of his *Antiquities*, and finally in his autobiography, *The Life*. As an admirer of Thucydides and Polybius, the grand historians of the Greco-Roman world, Josephus was a penetrative student of political power and a master of historical narrative. As a follower of the Pharisees, he was thoroughly versed in the teachings of the Written and the Oral Law and was himself a believer in the immortality of the soul and the resurrection of the body. As a committed Jew, he was highly sensitive to the sufferings and helplessness of the Jews, pressed in the grip of imperial Rome. Josephus is a precious source, revealing the Roman imperial system as it functioned in Jesus' day; the systems of Judaism prevalent at the time; the revolutionary spasms that convulsed the land; and the charismatics, prophets, and would-be messiahs who roamed the hills of Judea and Galilee.

Josephus's work lends itself to the ends we are seeking. From his writings we can construct the framework within which Jesus' life, trial, crucifixion, and resurrection were played out. But we can do even more. With Josephus as our guide, we may be able even to resurrect the historical Jesus who for so long has eluded us. By drawing a portrait of a charismatic of charismatics from the intricate web of time, place, structures, and linkages woven for us by Josephus, we may be in a position to compare this portrait with those drawn for us in the Gospels. Never was the time more ripe or more ready for a spirit capable of charting a trajectory from life to Life—a spirit whose earthly fate would not be his destiny.

Let us then set off on our odyssey from Who crucified Jesus? to What crucified Jesus?—an odyssey from human bitterness, hate, and blindness to divine love, reconciliation, and enlightenment.

RENDER UNTO CAESAR: IN ROME'S IMPERIAL GRIP

The Jewish people had been in the grip of Rome long before the time of Jesus. From that critical moment when the Roman general Pompey had stamped the seal of Rome on Hyrcanus II (63–40 B.C.), Jews had exercised little control over their land or their destiny. All who governed Jews, whether puppet kings like Herod (40–4 B.C.) or procurators like Pontius Pilate (A.D. 26–36), governed as instruments of the Roman imperium. And Rome's grip loosened not at all in the years that followed the trial and crucifixion of Jesus.

The imperial grip was painful but bearable during those early years when Hyracanus II and Herod retained the trappings of kingly power. It became less and less bearable in the waning years of Herod's reign, and the frustration, the bitterness, and the resentment of the people began to be expressed in strident defiance and violent demonstrations. It became intolerable when, after Herod's death, Rome dispensed with puppet kings and determined to rule Judea directly through procurators appointed by the emperor. From that moment on, the Jews were to know no peace, no serenity, no security until the Temple was in ruins, thousands lay slain, and thousands more had been carted off to Rome.

This epoch of violence was ushered in by an event that occurred on the eve of Herod's death. Some youthful firebrands, stirred by the urgings of two renowned sages, hacked down the golden eagle that Herod had erected over the great gate of the Temple. Apprehended and arrested, they were brought before Herod. When asked by whose orders they had cut down the eagle, they replied, "The Law of our Fathers." When Herod asked further why they were exultant when death was so imminent, they answered, "Because, after our death, we shall enjoy greater felicity." Enraged, Herod denounced these firebrands before the public assembly as sacrilegious persons who, under the pretext of zeal for the Law, had more ambitious aims in view, and he had them and the sages who had inspired them burnt alive (*The Jewish War* I: 648–55).

The anger of the people was not visible at the time of this tragic event. Herod's decision was accepted in silence. But immediately after Herod's death, large numbers gathered in the Temple area and began to bewail the fate of the young men. "This mourning," Josephus tells us,

> was in no subdued tones: there were piercing shrieks, a dirge directed by a conductor, and lamentations with beating of the breast, which resounded throughout the city. . . . These martyrs ought, they clamored, to be avenged by the punishment of Herod's favorites and . . . the deposition of the high priest whom he had appointed, as they had a right to select a man of greater piety and purer morals (*The Jewish War* II: 5–13).

All efforts by Herod's son, Archelaus, to still the clamor were of no avail. With Passover at hand and with the multitudes who were crowding in from the countryside being exposed to the agitations of those mourning for the martyred youths and their teachers, Archelaus was frightened and sent a cohort of troops to suppress the agitators. Indignant at the appearance of the troops, the crowd reacted with violence: They killed most of the soldiers and wounded the tribune in command. Terrified by this show of rebellion, Archelaus ordered his entire army into the city, with the result that three thousand lost their lives while others scattered to the neighboring hills (cf. *The Jewish War* II: 5–13).

The cutting down of the eagle, Herod's angry response, the violence of the mourners, and the harsh repression of the rioters by Archelaus all set the stage for the tragedies to come. The golden eagle was an especially sensitive issue. Was it equivalent to an image of the emperor and, as such, an affront to a core belief of Judaism? Or was it merely a symbol of loyalty to Rome? Herod, who viewed the eagle as merely a symbol of loyalty, was outraged. He had always respected the core tenets of Judaism and had demonstrated this respect by rebuilding the Temple in grand style. How, then, could he be accused of violating the Second Commandment? For him, the eagle was a symbol, pure and simple, and therefore those who were responsible for cutting it down could have been activated only by political motives. But for the two firebrands and their teachers, the golden eagle represented an image of the emperor and, as such, might have been looked upon as an object of divine worship.

The majority of the religious leaders seem to have sided with Herod's view since they did not challenge his right to execute the troublemakers. As for the people at large, some were so clearly outraged by what Herod had done that they reacted with violent demonstrations. Others may have deplored the execution of the malefactors even though they themselves looked upon the eagle as an innocuous symbol. However, the fact that there was no simple way to distinguish religious/nonpolitical action from religious/political action was bound to unleash violent reactions in the years that followed.

Not long after Archelaus had sounded the leitmotiv of violent repression, another fierce confrontation took place between Jews and Romans. A large number of Jews were so angered by the efforts of Sabinus, a Roman officer, to gain access to the royal treasures that they surrounded the Roman troops in the Temple precincts and engaged them in battle. So fierce was their attack that only the reinforcements led by Varus, the governor of Syria himself, finally subdued the outbreak, but not before Varus had set fire to the Temple porticoes. Large numbers of Jews were burned to death in the flames and still more were butchered by the soldiers. To underscore his determination to dampen the Jews' passion for violent confrontations with Roman authority, Varus *crucified* about two thousand of the most active insurrectionists and imprisoned a large number of the "less turbulent" (*The Jewish War* II: 66–75).

At the time these disruptive events were occurring, other upheavals were also disturbing the peace. In Galilee, Judas the son of Ezekias, a revolutionary from Herod's day, "raised a considerable body of followers, broke open the royal arsenals, and, having armed his companions, attacked the other aspirants to power" (*The Jewish War* II: 55–56).

Not to be outdone, in Peraea, a certain Simon crowned himself, perambulated the country with a band of revolutionaries, and burned down the royal palace at Jericho, along with many other stately mansions. "Not a house of any respectability," writes Josephus, "would have escaped the flames" had not Gratus, the commander of the royal infantry, decapitated Simon in a hand-to-hand encounter (*The Jewish War* II: 58–59).

Another aspirant to the throne, a shepherd by the name of Athrongaeus, donned a diadem and led raiding expeditions throughout the country. His victims, according to Josephus, were not only Romans and royalists but any wealthy Jews who had the misfortune to fall into his clutches. Only with difficulty did the authorities apprehend the leaders of these bandits (*The Jewish War* II: 60–65).

And while all this turbulence was rocking Judea, the emperor Augustus was giving ear to the various contenders for Herod's mantle and pondering whether Judea should continue to be governed by a puppet king, as Herod had been, or by a direct appointee from Rome. Augustus finally opted for direct rule. He reduced the territory of Archelaus, Herod's son, to a Roman province and sent out Coponius, a Roman of the equestrian order, to serve as procurator. Coponius was invested with full powers, including that of inflicting capital punishment.

Coponius ushered in the new dispensation with an act that set the teeth of the Jews on edge. As soon as he had taken office, he ordered a census and an assessment of Jewish property in order to determine the amount of tribute to be exacted. The Jews were shocked and inclined to resist. Only the pleas of the high priest deterred them from what would have been a tragic confrontation. But two sages, Judas of Galilee and Zadok the Pharisee, refused to knuckle under. They called on the people to revolt, insisting that God and God alone could be called *Despotes*, Emperor. It was blasphemous, they said, to obey the Roman emperor's decrees. "Heaven would be their zealous helper," they reassured the people, "to no lesser end than the furthering of their enterprise until it succeeded—all the more if with high devotion in their hearts they stood firm and did not shrink from the bloodshed that might be necessary" (*Antiquities* XVIII: 5–6).

The appeal of Judas and Zadok did not go unheeded. Indeed, so many flocked to their banner that they fathered within Judaism a Fourth Philosophy alongside the three philosophies already in existence—those of the Sadducees, the Pharisees, and the Essenes. Though adhering to Pharisaic teachings on all other issues, the followers of the Fourth Philosophy rejected the dictum of the Pharisees that the law of the emperor was to be obeyed as long as it did not violate any of the core teachings of Judaism.

Josephus tells us that the Fourth Philosophy attracted many followers. He also assures us that "these men sowed the seed of every kind of misery, which so afflicted the nation that words are inadequate [and that] when they had won an abundance of devotees, they filled the body politic immediately with tumult, also planting the seeds of those troubles that subsequently overtook it, all because of the novelty of this hitherto unknown philosophy" (*Antiquities* XVIII: 6; 9–10).

The rise of the Fourth Philosophy underscores the blurred line that separated the religious/nonpolitical realm from the religious/political realm. From the point of view of the founders of the Fourth Philosophy, the call for revolution against Rome was inspired by religious, not political, zeal. They claimed that it was blasphemous to call any individual *despotes*, lord, master, emperor. God and God alone was *Despotes*, Lord, Master, Emperor. Their call to arms was intended to overthrow another Antiochus who was challenging God's claim to be the only God. Such a call to arms had political consequences, but it was not motivated or justified on political grounds. The fact that both Judas and Zadok were sages, not soldiers, and the fact that Josephus dignified this revolutionary movement by setting it beside the schools of thought of the Sadducees, Pharisees, and Essenes as another religious philosophy within Judaism attest to the religious wellsprings of this violent challenge to Rome.

From the point of view, however, of the high priest Joazar and from the point of view of the leading spokesmen for the Pharisees, the taking of a census, the assessment of property, and the payment of tribute fell within Caesar's domain. For them, paying tribute to the emperor was not equivalent to paying tribute to a god.

Thus when Pontius Pilate entered on his procuratorship in A.D. 26 and immediately reconfirmed Caiaphas as high priest, he fell heir to a country that had been wracked by continuous violence from the moment the youths had torn down the golden eagle. Judea was clearly no sinecure. It was, rather, a battleground where the mettle of the procurator and his high priest was put to the test day in and day out. If Pontius Pilate were to make his mark and show himself worthy of advancement in the hierarchy of imperial power, it was essential that he impress the emperor with his ability to maintain law and order in a land that had proven itself to be a seedbed of dissidence, disorder, and violence. Tiberius (A.D. 14–37), who had succeeded Augustus as emperor and had appointed Pilate, was scarcely in the mood for a repetition of the years of turbulence that had shaken Judea after the death of Herod. Unless Pontius Pilate was shrewd enough to govern this unruly people, his tenure as procurator was bound to be extremely short.

The nub of Pontius Pilate's problem was where to draw the line between the legitimate rights of the Jews to exercise religious autonomy—rights that the Roman emperors themselves had granted—and the illegitimate stretching of those rights to the point at which they became religious justifications or pretexts for challenging Roman authority. Such a line, however, was not an easy one to draw. Was the Roman eagle a symbol of loyalty to Rome or was it an object of worship? Were the Jews merely demanding their religious rights when they equated the golden eagle with busts of the emperor or did their objection mask a political challenge, thinly veiled by a religious pretext?

Whereas the affair of the golden eagle did not lend itself to easy categorization, the ideology of the Fourth Philosophy offered no such ambiguity. From the outset, Judas of Galilee and Zadok the Pharisee had made no bones about the political consequences of their insistence that only God could be called *Despotes.* Even though this insistence was religious in appeal and motivation, it could not be acted upon without defying Roman political authority. One who heeded the religious call of Judas and Zadok must refuse to pay taxes to Rome, an act of disobedience that the Romans could not possibly allow to be disguised as an appeal to religious autonomy. Furthermore, since their defiance went hand in hand with a call for a violent uprising against the Romans and their Jewish collaborators, there was no question that the followers of the Fourth Philosophy had crossed the line that separated religious from political turf.

Pontius Pilate, confronted as he was with the need to make tough decisions and concerned as he was with exacting the required tribute, needed to impress the people with his toughness and yet avoid the need for force majeure. He therefore gingerly experimented with a point where he might safely draw the line. His first experiment was a failure; the second was a success. Here is Josephus's account of Pilate's first test of the people's mettle:

> Pilate, being sent by . . . Tiberius as procurator to Judea, introduced into Jerusalem by night and under cover the effigies of Caesar, which are called standards. This proceeding, when day broke, aroused immense excitement among the Jews; those who were on the spot were in consternation, *considering their laws to have been trampled underfoot* as those laws permit no image to be erected in the city; while the indignation of the townspeople stirred the country folk, who flocked together in crowds. Hastening after Pilate to Caesarea, the Jews implored him to remove the standards from Jerusalem and to uphold the laws of their ancestors. When Pilate refused, they fell prostrate around his house and for five whole days and nights remained motionless in that position.
>
> On the ensuing day Pilate took his seat on his tribunal in the great stadium and summoning the multitude, with the apparent intention of answering them, gave the arranged signal to his armed soldiers to surround the Jews. Finding themselves in a ring of troops three deep, the Jews were struck dumb at this unexpected sight. Pilate, after threatening to cut them down if they refused to admit Caesar's images, signaled to the soldiers to draw

> their swords. Thereupon the Jews, as by concerted action, flung themselves in a body on the ground, extended their necks, and exclaimed that they were ready rather to die than to transgress the Law. Overcome with astonishment at such intense religious zeal, Pilate gave orders for the immediate removal of the standards (*The Jewish War* II: 169–174; emphasis mine).

However, Pilate's second experiment proved more successful:

> On a later occasion he provoked a fresh uproar by expending upon the construction of an aqueduct the sacred treasure known as *Corbanas* [Greek transliteration from the Hebrew word meaning "sacrifices"]; the water was brought from a distance of 400 furlongs. Indignant at this proceeding, the populace formed a ring around the tribunal of Pilate, then on a visit to Jerusalem, and besieged him with angry clamor. He, foreseeing the tumult, had interspersed among the crowd a troop of soldiers, armed but disguised in civilian dress, with orders not to use their swords but to beat any rioters with cudgels. He now from his tribunal gave the agreed signal. Large numbers of the Jews perished, some from the blows that they received, others trodden to death by their companions in the ensuing flight. Cowed by the fate of the victims, the multitude was reduced to silence (*The Jewish War* II: 175–77).

It is evident that Pilate's sacrilegious act angered the people. It is also evident that they did not regard this sacrilege as one that must be resisted by martyrdom. Pilate as a plunderer of the Temple treasury was guilty of outright robbery and disrespect, but he was not guilty of imposing idolatrous images upon the Jews. Hence his show of strength was sufficient to cow Jewish resistance.

Pontius Pilate and the people at large thus, early on, knew where they stood with each other. Pilate had been forewarned that any tampering with an *essential* belief of the Jewish people would be resisted with martyrdom. On the other hand, if his provocations fell short of such tampering, the people would give way to coercive pressure.

It is evident from Josephus's account that Pontius Pilate was shrewd, tough, ruthless, and successful. His ten years in office testified to his good record in the preserving of law and order. He was able to head off trouble before it reached dangerous proportions. *His key to effective governance was to nip revolutions in the bud by making no distinction between "political" and "religious" dissidents. Dissidence, not motive or rallying cry, was his target.* For him, a charismatic's vision of the kingdom of God as one that God himself would usher in was equally as threatening as the revolutionaries' call to rise up against the Romans, for the end result would be the same: Roman rule would be finished. For Pilate, the beginning of wisdom was the fear of revolt, however masked by religious pietudes.

But Pilate could not achieve his objectives unless there were a loyal and able Jewish counterpart as committed to Pilate's strategy as was Pilate himself. In Caiaphas, he found such a counterpart. No previous high priest had ever held this high office for such a long period of time, and no subsequent high priest was ever to best Caiaphas's record. This was no mean achievement. Every procurator, both prior to and following Pontius Pilate, was free to employ a pliant high priest. Since Herod's day, the high priest had been appointed and dismissed at the whim of the ruler. The high priest's sacred robes were kept under lock and key by the political authorities, to be released only on festivals when he needed them in order to perform his duties. *Held thus firmly in the grip of puppet king or procurator, all high priests had to toe the line.*

Yet Caiaphas seems to have been the only high priest who possessed those special qualities that enabled him to serve not just one but two procurators. Since he held the office for a full ten years under such a demanding procurator as Pontius Pilate, Caiaphas obviously had the ability to keep the anger of the people from boiling over into violent anti-Roman demonstrations. This was no easy task when we bear in mind that it was Caiaphas who was the high priest when Pilate aroused the wrath of the people by bringing the effigies of the emperor into Jerusalem, and also when he robbed the Temple treasury to build an aqueduct. Yet Caiaphas weathered the storms and held his post throughout Pilate's administration. No major disturbances marred their relationship—an eloquent testimony to the high priest's skill in snuffing out sparks before they burst into flames.

There was one event, however, during the high priesthood of

Caiaphas that reveals the fear and trembling in high places. Although this event occurred outside the political jurisdiction of Pontius Pilate, it reflects the cast of mind of all who exercised authority during those discordant and troublesome times. It involved a charismatic, John the Baptist, who was put to death by Herod the Tetrarch.

Here is Josephus's account of the occurrence and of the motives that prompted the ruler's violent reaction:

> But to some of the Jews the destruction of Herod's army seemed to be divine vengeance, and certainly a just vengeance, for his treatment of John, surnamed the Baptist. For Herod had put him to death, though he was a good man and had exhorted the Jews to lead righteous lives, to practice justice toward their fellows and piety toward God, and [in] so doing to join in baptism. In his view, this was a necessary preliminary if baptism was to be acceptable to God. They must not employ it to gain pardon for whatever sins they committed but as a consecration of the body, implying that the soul was already thoroughly cleansed by right behavior. When others, too, joined the crowds about him because they were aroused to the highest degree by his sermons, Herod became alarmed. *Eloquence that had so great an effect on mankind might lead to some form of sedition* for it looked as if they would be guided by John in everything they did.
>
> *Herod decided, therefore, that it would be much better to strike first and be rid of him before his work led to an uprising than to wait for an upheaval, get involved in a difficult situation, and see his mistake.* Though John, because of Herod's suspicions, was brought in chains to Marchaerus [a stronghold] and there put to death, yet the verdict of the Jews was that the destruction visited upon Herod's army was a vindication of John, since God saw fit to inflict such a blow on Herod (*Antiquities* XVIII: 116–119; emphasis mine).

Josephus had little sympathy for Jews who sought to overthrow Roman rule. Yet he was not at all pleased with rulers who provoked the people unnecessarily by clamping down on religious zealots and ardent preachers, especially when, as in the case of John, their preaching was aimed at stirring the people to cleanse themselves of their sins, not of their rulers. John, in Josephus's opinion, was a good man who exhorted the Jews to live righteous lives, to practice justice toward their fellows and piety toward God. When John called the people to join him in baptism, he was urging them to participate in a symbolic act signifying that their souls had already been cleansed by the righteous lives they had lived since heeding his call. There was nothing political in John's teachings. He was a religious charismatic—pure and simple.

Yet, as Josephus points out, Herod the Tetrarch was unwilling to accept John for what he was. As long as crowds were aroused by John's sermons, the ruler feared that such eloquence could stir the people to some form of sedition. For John was no ordinary preacher. He could so stir his listeners with his aura that they would willingly follow wherever he might lead. Thus Herod was confronted with a dilemma: If he ignored John, the crowds might become more and more prone to violence in response to some real or imagined provocation. On the other hand, if he put John to death, he might be inviting the very outbreak he was attempting to avoid. It turned out that, in this instance at least, Herod the Tetrarch had made a shrewd decision: The people, though aroused and angry, did not rise up.

The Roman imperial framework, within which Jesus' life, preaching, trial, crucifixion, and attested resurrection took place, is clear enough. At the pinnacle of power and authority was the emperor, who exercised his authority over the Jews either through puppet kings, like Herod, or through procurators, like Coponius and Pontius Pilate. These imperial instruments, in turn, sought to carry out their responsibilities to the emperor by appointing high priests, who were selected for their pliancy rather than their piety. Their function was to serve as the eyes and ears of the puppet king or procurator, so as to head off demonstrative challenges to Roman rule. Of these high priests, only one—Caiaphas—had such piercing eyes and such keen ears that he was able to keep the confidence of the procurators he served as long as they remained in office.

But even Caiaphas could scarcely have done his job singlehandedly. It is thus highly likely that he appointed a council, or sanhedrin, consisting of individuals who were well aware of the dire consequences that would follow any outbreak against Roman authority, however innocent and naive its instigator. To be sure, such a sanhedrin is not specifically mentioned by Josephus in his account of the incumbency of Pontius Pilate and Caiaphas. But he does mention such a sanhedrin when he tells us of the trial and stoning of James, the brother of Jesus, during the procuratorship of Albinus and the high priesthood of Ananus:

> The younger Ananus, who . . . had been appointed to the high priesthood, was rash in his temper and unusually daring. He followed the school of the Sadducees, who are indeed more heartless than any of the other Jews . . . when they sit in judgment.
>
> Possessed of such a character, Ananus thought that he had a favorable opportunity because Festus was dead and Albinus [the new procurator] was still on the way. And so he convened a sanhedrin of judges and brought before them a man named James, the brother of Jesus who was called the Christ, and certain others. He accused them of having transgressed the law and delivered them up to be stoned.
>
> *Those of the inhabitants of the city who were considered the most fair-minded and who were strict in the observance of the law were offended at this.* They therefore secretly sent to King Agrippa urging [that he order Ananus] to desist from any further actions. Certain of them even went to meet Albinus, who was on his way from Alexandria, and informed him that Ananus had no authority to convene a sanhedrin without his consent. Convinced by these words, Albinus angrily wrote to Ananus threatening to take vengeance upon him. King Agrippa, because of Ananus's action, deposed him from the high priesthood, which he had held for three months, and replaced him with Jesus the son of Damnaeus (*Antiquities* XX: 197–203; emphasis mine).

Josephus's account of the stoning of James is of vital importance for it reveals the role of the high priest as being that of the procurator's procurator. It also reveals the thin line that separated the religious from the political realm. Ananus, Josephus tells us, was a high priest and a Sadducee. Taking advantage of the brief period when there was no procurator in Jerusalem, Ananus acted as though he himself were the procurator. He not only convened a sanhedrin but he had James stoned to death on the grounds that he had violated the law. This act, however, aroused such bitter opposition from those who were strict in their observance of the laws—the Scribes-Pharisees[2]—that they informed King Agrippa of Ananus's illegal action. Others reminded Albinus that *Ananus had no right to convene a sanhedrin in the absence of the procurator.* Whereupon King Agrippa lost no time in deposing Ananus from the high priesthood.

The striking point here is that Ananus was a Sadducee. He thus could not possibly have seen eye to eye with the Pharisees on matters of religious law. The Sadducees believed that God had revealed the Written Law only, while the Pharisees taught that God had provided for two Laws, a Written Law *and* an Oral Law. *The Pharisees could not have participated in a sanhedrin if a judgment were to be made on the basis of religious law, even though they could participate in a sanhedrin if the basis of judgment were to be political.*

James's preaching may have been deemed politically dangerous by the high priest, even though the message was couched in religious language. *But James's preaching clearly was not deemed political by the strict observers of the religious laws, the Pharisees.* They were appalled at Ananus's harsh and illegal judgment and took steps to have him removed from office.

Throughout this passage, Josephus assumes that the sanhedrin that Ananus convened was a sort of privy council, not a permanent body that enjoyed a religious status independent of the high priest and procurator. It is thus evident that, whatever the religious commitments of the members of this council may have been, when they served on the high priest's council, they served as political, not religious, advisers.

That the sanhedrin was a privy council and not a religious body is further confirmed by Josephus when he recounts the episode in which Agrippa granted the Levites the right to wear linen garments, as he did the priests:

[2]After much research I am convinced that although in the Greek and Roman translations of the Gospels they are treated as referring to separate classes, the terms *Scribe* and *Pharisee* are synonymous. (See Rivkin, "Scribes-Pharisees, Lawyers, Hypocrites: A Study in Synonymity," *Hebrew College Annual* 49 [1978]).

> The Levites . . . , who were singers of hymns, urged the king to convene a sanhedrin and get them permission to wear linen robes on equal terms with the priests. . . . The king, with the consent of those who attended the sanhedrin, allowed the singers of hymns to discard their former robes and to wear linen ones such as they wished. Those in the tribe who served in the Temple were also permitted to learn the hymns by heart, as they had requested. All this was contrary to the ancestral laws, and such transgression was bound to make us liable to punishment (*Antiquities* XX: 216–18). [We are dealing here with a break from custom, not law, since Levites are not prohibited from wearing linen. At the same time, there was no law that, as was the case with the priests, commanded them to wear linen. But as students of religion know only too well, any deviation from a traditional mode or practice can wound religious sensitivities, even when such a deviation is not from law but from precedent and custom.]

It is evident from our reading of Josephus that King Agrippa had the right to convoke a sanhedrin—a privy council—to advise him with respect to an issue that lay within his *political* jurisdiction—that is, the Temple and its management. *We are therefore not dealing with a sanhedrin that possessed some permanent religious or political status but rather with a privy council that functioned as an adjunct to the political authority.*

Indeed, when Josephus uses the term *sanhedrin* in his writings, *it always refers to a council appointed by an emperor, a king, or a high priest.* He *never* uses the term when he is speaking of a permanent legislative body such as the Roman senate. Such a body he usually calls a *boulé.* Thus whenever Herod wished to have one of his sons, wives, or other relatives put to death for treason, he would convoke a sanhedrin, not a *boulé.* Such a sanhedrin based its judgment on political, not religious, grounds. Similarly, when Josephus tells us of Herod's trial and uses the term *sanhedrin,* it is because Herod was being tried for overstepping his political, not his religious, authority. Sameias and Pollion, both Pharisees, participated in that sanhedrin, but they were sitting on a sanhedrin as powerful leaders concerned with *political* issues, *not* as religious leaders intending to judge Herod on religious grounds.

Although Josephus does not specifically mention that Caiaphas convoked a sanhedrin, this does not mean that Caiaphas did not have a privy council; for Josephus says nothing about Caiaphas's priesthood, other than that he was the high priest. We may therefore assume that if Caiaphas had had to deal with a charismatic such as Jesus, he would have been willing to render a judgment without taking counsel with a sanhedrin, his privy council, which had only a political, not a religious, function.

A close reading of Josephus has provided us with the political framework within which the life, ministry, trial, crucifixion, and witnessed resurrection of Jesus were played out. This is the framework presupposed by the Gospels, Acts, and the Epistles of Paul. The Roman emperor ruled Judea, Galilee, and Samaria by means of puppet kings, governors, procurators, and procurator-appointed high priests. But the Jewish people over whom these instruments ruled proved to be ungovernable.

In such a world, where violence stalked the countryside, death frequented the streets of Jerusalem, and riots disturbed the precincts of the Temple; where every flutter of dissidence sent chills of fear up the spines of puppet kings, governors, procurators, and procurator-appointed high priests, even the most nonpolitical of charismatics took his life in his hands when he preached the good news of God's coming kingdom. And if his call to repentance were so eloquent that crowds gathered round to hear and to hope, would not the power of his word invite the kiss of death?

RENDER UNTO GOD: THE MOSAIC OF JUDAISM

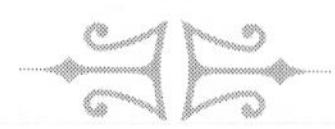

Judea was under the control of Rome. The emperor, the procurator, the high priest, and the high priest's privy council all were tied together by two interests: the preservation of imperial power in the face of any challenge and the smooth collection of tribute for the enrichment of Rome. All those who functioned in the imperial interest were not motivated by religious but by political considerations. The high priest was no exception, even though he ministered in the Temple and he alone was allowed to enter the Holy of Holies on the Day of Atonement to seek God's forgiveness for the sins of all Israel. Yet he himself was, in the sight of God, an arch sinner, for nowhere in the Five Books of Moses or in the repository of the Oral Law, the Mishnah, do we read that a high priest is to be an appointee of any king, prince, or potentate. According to the Pentateuch, the high priesthood was to be reserved for the direct lineal descendants of Aaron, Eleazar, and Phineas.

From the standpoint of God's Law, all high priests who held office since Herod's day were illegitimate. They had been merely political instruments imposed by regal power and acquiesced to by the leaders of the three divergent forms of Judaism in Jesus' day—the Judaism of the Sadducees, of the Pharisees, and of the Essenes. Though the followers of each of these forms regarded the followers of the others as heretics and rejecters of God's will, Judaism appeared to the Roman authorities as a mosaic with three inlays, which, though distinguishable one from another, were nonetheless of a single design. And this was so because, out of desperation, the leaders of each form had committed themselves to two doctrines:

the doctrine of the two realms to regulate their relationship to the state and the doctrine of live and let live to regulate their relationship to one another. In a word, they urged their followers to render unto Caesar what was Caesar's so that they would be able to render unto God what was God's. And they also, in order to exist amiably side by side with one another, had initiated a policy of peaceful coexistence.

Let us now take a closer look at each of the three inlays—the Sadducees, the Pharisees, and the Essenes—so that we can comprehend how three such divergent forms of Judaism could have appeared to the Roman authorities as a mosaic rather than as separate, distinct, and mutually exclusive forms of the religion of Israel. For at first glance, the differences that set them apart were far more impressive and fundamental than those that drew them together.

The Sadducees believed that God had revealed one Law only—the Five Books of Moses; the Scribes-Pharisees believed that God had revealed two Laws—one Written and the other Oral; while the Essenes believed that God had also revealed his will in books besides the Pentateuch and the other books of the Bible. There were additional significant differences as well: The Sadducees believed that God had endowed Aaron and his sons with absolute authority over God's Law and over his cultus; the Scribes-Pharisees believed that God had endowed first Moses, then Joshua, then the elders, then the prophets, and then themselves with absolute authority over God's twofold Law, the Written and the Oral; while the Essenes kept themselves aloof from the people at large and from the cultus of the day. And finally, while the Sadducees believed that God rewarded the righteous and punished the wicked in this world, the Scribes-Pharisees believed that God rewarded the righteous with eternal life for the soul and resurrection for the body and that he punished the souls of the wicked with eternal suffering in the nether world. As for the Essenes, they believed that the souls of the righteous would enjoy eternal life, but they did not believe in the resurrection of the body. But however severe and tenacious their differences, the Sadducees, Scribes-Pharisees, and Essenes all looked to God, not to the Roman emperor, as their Lord.

Whereas the procurator-appointed high priest and his privy council were harnessed to the imperial chariot, the Sadducees, Pharisees, and Essenes were yoked to God.

In Jesus' day the Scribes-Pharisees were the most luminous inlay within the mosaic of Judaism. It was they who sat in Moses' seat, and it was they who determined the norms by which all public religious functions were carried out in accordance with the provisions of the Written and Oral Law. Thus the religious calendar of the Temple followed the lunar-solar calendar of the Oral Law. The sacrifices in the Temple and the celebrations of the festivals were carried out in accordance with the Oral Law. In a word, the Oral Law of the Scribes-Pharisees was normative for all Jews insofar as public manifestations of religion were concerned. The religious activity of the Sadducees and Essenes was confined to their private domains, and their religious teachings were restricted to doctrinal claims and verbal protestations.

It had not always been thus. The Scribes-Pharisees had not always sat in Moses' seat. In fact, they had been sitting there only since the Hasmonean revolt (167–142 B.C.). Before that time, the Scribes-Pharisees had not even existed: Those in authority had belonged to the Aaronide priesthood, presided over by a high priest who traced his descent from Aaron, Eleazar, Phineas, and Zadok. The Aaronide priesthood had administered the Written Law. The rewards and punishments they proclaimed to the people were this-worldly. Their religious calendar was not geared to the moon but to the sun. All public worship was carried out precisely as Moses had prescribed in the Pentateuch. No other class either had or sought authority over the Law. The scribes in those days had been intellectuals who pursued Wisdom, not power, and they heaped praises on the high priest and his fellow Aaronides. They were not the Scribes-Pharisees of Jesus' day.

These Scribes-Pharisees were newcomers. They had burst out in response to the crisis that Antiochus Epiphanes precipitated when he launched his drive to hellenize and polytheize the Jews. By expelling Onias II from the high priestly office and exiling him to Egypt and by appointing first Jason and then Meneleus in his stead, Antiochus had violated the provisions laid down by the Pentateuch for the high priestly succession. And by his insistence that, on pain of death, Jews must worship Zeus and abandon their God-given laws, Antiochus compelled them to weigh the consequences of martyrdom, since the Pentateuch confined rewards and punishment to this world. If one obeyed the Law, one died; if one disobeyed, one lived. Thus in the train of these events, there opened up a leadership gap and a doctrinal gap—gaps that the Scribes-Pharisees jumped in to bridge.

They bridged the leadership gap by seating themselves in Moses' seat, and they bridged the doctrinal gap by proclaiming that God had given two Laws, the Written and the Oral, not the Written only; and that God had promised eternal life for the soul and resurrection for the body to each individual who adhered to this twofold Law. Martyrdom would not end in death, as the Pentateuch implied, but in life eternal.

Many years after this good news was proclaimed by the Scribes-Pharisees, Josephus held up this belief as the great prize that awaited every Jew who loyally adhered to the twofold Law:

> For those . . . who live in accordance with our laws the prize is not silver or gold, no crown of wild olive or of parsley or with any such public mark of distinction. No; each individual, relying on the witness of his own conscience and the lawgiver's prophecy, confirmed by the sure testimony of God, is firmly persuaded that to those who observe the laws and if they must need die for them willingly meet death, God has granted a renewed existence and in the revolution of the ages the gift of a better life.
>
> I should have hesitated to write thus had not the facts made all men aware that many of our countrymen have on many occasions ere now preferred to have all manner of suffering rather than utter a single word against the Law (*Against Apion* II: 217b–19).

Josephus pictures the glorious life after death of the righteous in another passage:

> Know you not that they who depart this life in accordance with the law of nature and repay the loan [of the soul] that they received from God, when he who lent is pleased to reclaim it, win eternal renown; that their houses and families are secure; that their souls, remaining spotless and obedient, are allotted the

> most holy place in heaven, whence in the revolution of the ages, they return to find in chaste bodies a new habitation?
>
> But as for those who have laid mad hands on themselves [and committed suicide], the darker regions of the nether world receive their souls, and God, their Father, visits upon their posterity the outrageous acts of the parents (*The Jewish War* III: 374–75).

That the souls of the deserving will enjoy the nearness of God the Father is foreshadowed by the words Josephus puts in Abraham's mouth as the Patriarch readies himself to sacrifice his son Isaac:

> "Aye, since thou wast born [out of the course of nature, so] quit thou now this life not by the common road but sped by thine own father on thy way to God, the Father of all, through the rites of sacrifice. He, I ween, accounts it not meant for thee to depart this life by sickness or war or by any of the calamities that commonly befall mankind *but amid prayers and sacrificial ceremonies would receive thy soul and keep it near to himself*; and for me thou shalt be a protector and stay of my old age—to which end above all I nurtured thee—by giving me God instead of thyself."
>
> The son of such a father could not but be brave-hearted, and Isaac received these words with joy (*Antiquities* I: 228–32; emphasis mine).

This was good news indeed. God the Father loved each and every individual so much that he had revealed his twofold Law to Israel so that each individual who internalized this Law and adhered to it could look forward to eternal life for the soul and resurrection for the body. Uplifted by teachings as intoxicating as these, the overwhelming majority of the Jewish people gladly followed the teachings of the Scribes-Pharisees and happily acknowledged their right to sit in Moses' seat.

Not so the previous Aaronide leaders. They denounced this new class of Scribes as Perushim (*pharisaio* when transliterated into the Greek; hence the English Pharisees)—that is, separatists, deviants, heretics. When, in 142 B.C. a Great Synagogue invested Simon the Hasmonean with the high priesthood even though he was not a direct descendant of Aaron-Eleazar-Phineas-Zadok, the old priestly leaders proclaimed that only a Zadokite could be allowed to serve as high priest. The high priestly Aaron-Eleazar-Phineas line had been spelled out by Moses himself, and from the time Zadok had served as high priest in Solomon's Temple, the high priesthood had been exclusively the prerogative of his descendants. Those who justified a break from this line were violators of God's Law, for nowhere in the Pentateuch is a Great Synagogue mentioned, much less authorized to seat or unseat a high priest. Those who justified a non-Pentateuchal body and those who justified the investiture of a non-Zadokite as high priest on the grounds of an Oral Law could not be Soferim (respected Scribes as Ben Sira had been) but were usurpers, separatists, deviants, *pharisaio*—guilty of defying the clear, plain, and unambiguous words written down by Moses at God's command. Those who resisted the claims of this class came to be called the Zedukkim—that is, Sadducees.

The Sadducees' denunciations, however, were not heeded by the overwhelming majority of the Jewish people. For them, the good news of eternal life and resurrection preached by the Scribes-Pharisees proved far more alluring than the literal reading of Scripture by the Sadducees. Therefore, from the time of their triumphant ascendancy during the Hasmonean revolt until the time of Jesus and beyond, the Scribes-Pharisees sat securely in Moses' seat. Even when John Hyrcanus (135–105 B.C.) broke with the Pharisees and abrogated the oral laws, the mass of people clung to the Scribes-Pharisees. And when Alexander Janneus (102–76 B.C.) persisted in negating the oral laws, the people at large rose up in violent revolt and refused to give in until Salome Alexandra (76–67 B.C.) reinstituted the oral laws and restored the Scribes-Pharisees to their dominant role. Aside from this violent interlude, the Oral Law of the Scribes-Pharisees, called *Halachah* in Hebrew, spelled out the norms by which all public manifestation of religion was conducted and by which the majority of Jews regulated their personal lives.

Although neither John Hyrcanus nor Alexander Janneus succeeded in their efforts to break the power of the Pharisees, they did succeed in forcing them to come to terms with the realities of political and religious power. Having suffered the brutalities of civil war and fearing such strife as a way of life, the Scribes-Pharisees were ready to accommodate themselves to the stubborn realities of this world by according recognition to the state as an independent entity and by according the Sadducees and the Essenes exemption from the provisions of the Oral Law insofar as this-worldly sanctions were concerned. This twofold accommodation to the specter of civil war was made manifest in the two doctrines mentioned: the doctrine of the two realms and the doctrine of live and let live.

Let us take a closer look at the way these doctrines evolved and functioned during the latter years of Hasmonean rule and beyond. As for the doctrine of the two realms, having suffered grievously from the indecisive civil war throughout the reign of Alexander Janneus, the Scribes-Pharisees had a strong interest in a peaceful settlement with the Hasmoneans. Although under Salome Alexandra the Pharisees once again enjoyed a degree of political power, by the end of her reign they came to recognize that the political arena was not their stage—that they were religious teachers whose power came from their preaching of the good news of eternal life and resurrection and from the love and respect they inspired in the masses. Convinced that this world was transient and that earthly satisfactions were of little moment, they focused their minds on the world to come, which would be eternal and fully satisfying.

Since the trappings of worldly power had no hold over them, the Scribes-Pharisees were willing to make a compact with their rulers, a compact that would accord to each realm its due. If the political authorities would agree to recognize the right of the Scribes-Pharisees to teach the twofold Law, determine the norms of public manifestations of religion and the liturgical calendar, and preach the good news of eternal life and resurrection, then the Scribes-Pharisees, for their part, would acknowledge the right of the political authorities to impose taxes, raise armies, fight wars, and administer the nonreligious areas of economic, social, and political life. In a word, the Scribes-Pharisees enunciated the doctrine of the legitimacy of two realms, the secular and the religious.

This doctrine proved to be attractive to the secular/political authorities. Thus they were willing to grant religious autonomy to the Scribes-Pharisees. The implications of this doctrine, however, were to have momentous consequences for accepting it meant nothing less than a promise on the part of the Scribes-Pharisees that as long as their religious autonomy was not violated, the political authorities were to be given a free hand.

This compact had its beginnings during the reign of Salome Alexandra. It was crystallized and activated after her death when the Scribes-Pharisees withdrew from the political arena. It was sustained throughout Herod's reign and reinforced when the procurators took over. In confirming the right of the procurator to collect tribute, the Scribes-Pharisees were translating their doctrine of the two realms—from rendering unto the king what is the king's and unto God what is God's—to its new formulation: Render unto Caesar what is Caesar's and unto God what is God's.

The doctrine of the two realms thus proved to be an eminently satisfying solution for the Scribes-Pharisees. They could more and more wash their hands of dirty politics, palace intrigues, and repressive measures to concentrate on saving souls. Even when they were consulted by the political authorities, the responsibility for decision making lay squarely in the hands of those authorities and not in the hands of the Scribes-Pharisees. Such decisions were political, not religious. The Scribes-Pharisees were consulted only because they had the trust of the people and could be counted on to fulfill their end of the contract—remind their followers that the secular rulers must be obeyed as long as they did not obstruct the road to eternal life and resurrection.

This the Scribes-Pharisees could do with a clear conscience. Their teachings had never promised the people a garden of roses in this world—only in the world to come. God's justice could not be weighed and measured by earthly felicity or by earthly pain and suffering. Indeed, without trials and tribulations, how was God to distinguish the sturdy righteous from those whose righteousness waxed and waned with the rewards and punishments of each passing day? Suffering—whether at the hands of the Hasmoneans, at the hands of the Herodians, or at the hands of the procurators—was thus no justification for either revolt or for railing at God's unconcern. Rather, it was a challenge to one's faith, a trial of one's beliefs, and a goad to one's righteousness. Suffering must be endured with resolute patience and stoic calm as long as the political authorities did not close off the glory road to everlasting life.

But should the political authorities fail to stay within their realm, should they trespass on the realm of the holy and sacred, then the people must rise up in revolt, as they had done when John Hyrcanus and Alexander Janneus had barred the road to eternal life. Or they could resort to passive resistance, willing to martyr themselves rather than yield. This they had indeed done when they refused to be cowed by Pontius Pilate's threats against them if they persisted in blocking the introduction of the emperor's images into Jerusalem and into the Temple.

The doctrine of the two realms proved to be a fruitful one. The political rulers, whether Hasmoneans, Herodians, or Romans, treated the Scribes-Pharisees with respect and, with the rarest of exceptions, did not obstruct their teachings, or tamper with their laws, or threaten their institutions. Thus Herod had released two Pharisaic sages, Sameias and Pollion, along with their disciples, from the need to take a loyalty oath to him. Contrariwise, Herod appealed successfully to the leaders of the Scribes-Pharisees when the firebrands tore down the golden eagle. Similarly, the most prestigious Pharisees were called upon by the political authorities to urge the people not to revolt against Rome even after the provocations of the procurator had become intolerable (*The Jewish War* II: 411–14). All these instances bespeak a trust: The Scribes-Pharisees would keep their side of the contract as long as the political rulers kept theirs.

This compact was reaffirmed when Coponius, having been appointed procurator after Herod's death, ordered the census to serve as the basis for the exaction of the imperial tribute. This order, as we have seen, was so bitterly resented by the people that it could easily have sparked a revolt had not the Scribes-Pharisees stood firmly behind their compact. The exaction of tribute fell in Caesar's domain. It did not bar the road to eternal life. The census-taking was a legitimate exercise of Roman authority and could *not* be challenged on *religious* grounds, no matter how much suffering and hardship the exaction of tribute would impose upon the people. The census was legal, the tribute was legal, its exaction was legal because Roman sovereignty was legal. It was legal because the doctrine of the two realms accorded unto Caesar all that was Caesar's and unto God all that was God's.

The Scribes-Pharisees' adherence to their compact was not

without heavy cost. For the first time since they had taken possession of Moses' seat, they found their leadership rejected by a significant number of their followers when Judas and Zadok denounced Coponius's order as being an affront to God's sovereignty. So fundamental indeed was this split with the Scribes-Pharisees that the Fourth Philosophy came to be recognized as a distinctive form of Judaism, like that of the Scribes-Pharisees, the Sadducees, and the Essenes.

As for the doctrine of live and let live, the Scribes-Pharisees of Jesus' day had long since given up their earlier efforts to bind the Sadducees to the Oral Law. Except for worship in the Temple, adherence to the religious calendar, and conformance to public ceremonial acts of a religious nature, the private acts and teachings of the Sadducees and their followers had come to be regarded as their own affair. Conflicts between Scribes-Pharisees and Sadducees were now confined exclusively to doctrinal debate. On a day-to-day basis, Scribes-Pharisees and Sadducees mingled freely, and Sadducean high priests carried out their Temple functions in accordance with the prescriptions of the oral laws with seeming good grace. Indeed, on such issues as political sovereignty, the Scribes-Pharisees and Sadducees tended to see eye to eye, since the Sadducees, like the Scribes-Pharisees, had committed themselves to the doctrine of the two realms. As long as the political authorities did not violate the fundamental principles of the Written Law that there is only one God, that no image of that God may be worshiped, and that sacrifices be offered up to God in his holy Temple, then as far as the Sadducees were concerned, there could be no challenge to the right of the political authorities to impose taxes, maintain law and order, and even to keep the garments of the high priest under lock and key.

So, too, the Scribes-Pharisees and Sadducees had agreed to a similar binding compact that regulated their relationship to each other. As long as the Sadducees carried out all public functions in accordance with Oral Law, the Scribes-Pharisees would raise no question to the right of a Sadducee to be high priest; or to the right of Sadducees to be priests and to enjoy all the honors, privileges, and revenues attendant to their priestly status; or to their right to live their private lives outside the jurisdiction of the Oral Law. The ultimate judgment was transferred from the hands of men to the hands of God. If, as the Scribes-Pharisees taught, God will punish with eternal suffering those who reject the twofold Law, the Sadducees would receive the punishment they deserved in the world to come. For their part, the Sadducees could anticipate that God would punish the Scribes-Pharisees for their heretical teachings by shortening their lives, visiting on them pain and suffering, withholding prosperity, and denying them the blessings of children in this world.

As long, then, as the ultimate sanctions were left to God, it was possible for Scribes-Pharisees and Sadducees to limit their doctrinal conflicts to acerbic debate. In many areas of mutual concern, especially those that might endanger the very existence of the people and the sanctuary, they could even collaborate. Of these areas, the most sensitive was the gray and murky area that lay between the religious realm and the political realm. For it was in this area that religious dissidence could not always be distinguished from political challenge—yet on this distinction, the life and death of the people hung precariously.

As for the Essenes, they, too, were subsumed under the compact of live and let live. As long as they kept to themselves and made no effort to gain control over the Temple cult, the Scribes-Pharisees and Sadducees were willing to let God decide what was to become of them.

It is thus evident that in Jesus' day, the Scribes-Pharisees and the Sadducees coexisted peacefully on the religious plane and held similar views on the political plane. Both had adopted a noninterference policy not only toward each other but toward every religious group in Judaism, however much it might deviate from their own beliefs. Whatever common concern they shared over religious dissidents whose teachings had dangerous political implications, such concern was political, not religious: Dissidents should be brought before some appropriate political authority—puppet king, procurator, or procurator-appointed high priest—to be judged on political grounds. Such dissidents were not brought before the Bet Din Hagadol (Great Boulé), the senate of the Scribes-Pharisees, or before any of their lesser bodies, each of which was called simply a *bet din* (*boulé*). In Jesus' day, these bodies did not exercise any political jurisdiction, while the religious jurisdiction they did exercise was limited to those Jews who voluntarily followed the teachings of the

Scribes-Pharisees. Adhering to their compact with the state, the Scribes-Pharisees steered clear of political involvement; and adhering to their compact with the Sadducees and Essenes, they confined their outrage at religious dissidents to verbal onslaughts. If, then, a charismatic stirred crowds with his call for repentance, awed crowds by his wonder-working, or uplifted crowds with the promise of God's kingdom to come, then the Scribes-Pharisees might confront him, they might remonstrate with him, they might even denounce him as an emissary of Beelzebul, but they would not—*for they could not*—arrest him and have him brought before either the Bet Din Hagadol or a lesser *bet din*. They could no more haul a charismatic before their religious bodies than they could haul the high priest Caiaphas, who, as a Sadducee, held far more outrageous religious beliefs than those held by many of the charismatics.

Thus the Judaism in Jesus' day, though it consisted of three distinctive facets blended together, appeared to the Romans as a mosaic rather than as separate and distinct insets. For though the Scribes-Pharisees, Sadducees, and Essenes looked upon one another as religious heretics, they all adhered to the doctrine of the two realms and the doctrine of live and let live. The Romans could therefore be certain that as long as they did not compel the Scribes-Pharisees, Sadducees, or Essenes to worship the emperor as a god or to install busts of the emperor in the Temple, and as long as the Romans did not interfere with their right to teach their distinctive doctrines, the leaders—whether of the Scribes-Pharisees, of the Sadducees, or of the Essenes—would urge their followers to be loyal to Rome, pay the tribute, and resist the blandishments of revolutionaries and charismatics, however couched in prophetic and pietistic language those blandishments might be. For the Romans, then, these three distinctive forms of Judaism formed a mosaic that flashed from all its facets the reassuring message: "Render unto Caesar the things that are Caesar's and unto God the things that are God's" (Mark 12:17).

FROM OUT OF THE DEPTHS THEY CRIED

The mosaic of Judaism was not fractured by the provocations of the ruling authorities. But many Jews found those provocations so painful that they could not submit passively. For them, the situation demanded some alternative to the doctrine of the two realms. It was inconceivable to them that God could be party to such harsh injustices. They believed that God could not and would not remain silent. Although the Pharisees, Sadducees, and Essenes may have drawn a line between the religious and secular realms, God had drawn no such line. Voices began to cry out that God was not neutral and that Caesar's realm was neither safe nor sacrosanct. These people believed that God's righteous justice would not be deterred by some imaginary line drawn by men, that God would bring low the haughtiness of emperors and wreak vengeance on their cruel injustices to God's people. Some believed the wrath of God would be manifested through violent revolutionaries. For others, God's wrath required no human instruments of violence; these people were drawn to charismatic teachers who proclaimed that the peaceful kingdom of God was at hand.

Those who were stirred to take the extreme revolutionary road had been inspired by the two sages Judas of Galilee and Zadok the Pharisee, who, as we have seen, had been aroused by the refusal of the Pharisaic leaders to regard the census as a religious issue and by their refusal to denounce the tribute. For Judas and Zadok, the issue was a religious one. They must throw down the gauntlet and take up arms against Rome. In this battle, God surely would lend power to those who were championing his cause and assure them victory.

This call to arms did not go unheeded. Many desperate Jews rallied around Judas and Zadok, confident that God was *not* neutral and that he would bless their violence with victory. These revolutionaries and their Fourth Philosophy gave the Romans and their Jewish collaborators no peace until their lives and their violence were snuffed out at Masada in the year A.D. 71.

The followers of the Fourth Philosophy, by rejecting the doctrine of the two realms, aroused the opposition not only of the Romans and their puppet high priests but also of the Pharisees, to whom they previously had been attached and to whose other doctrines they still adhered. But there was this difference: The Roman authorities and their Jewish surrogates countered violence with violence, while the Scribes-Pharisees confined their hostility to verbal denunciation and vilification. The Scribes-Pharisees exercised no coercive authority in the secular realm. Their authority was limited to public manifestations of religion—the liturgical calendar and the Temple ritual. Otherwise they adhered to their policy of noninterference. Sadducees and Essenes were not subjected to the *bet din*, the *boulé*, of the Scribes-Pharisees even though they rejected the twofold Law, and the same tolerance was extended to the Fourth Philosophy. Once Judas and Zadok broke from the Scribes-Pharisees, they were out of the jurisdiction of Pharisaic institutions. However much the Scribes-Pharisees may have denounced these leaders, however much they may have viewed the deaths of their followers at the hands of the Romans as a retribution from God, they themselves confined their hostility to verbal denunciations.

For the Roman authorities and the high priest, the Fourth Philosophy offered no real problem as to how it should be dealt with since its followers made no bones about their determination to overthrow Roman rule by force. Every effort to root them out, therefore, was deemed justified. Violence must be met with violence. The religious justification for their revolutionary ideology mattered neither to the Roman procurators nor to the high priests. As long as the Romans did not set up statues of the emperors in the Temple or parade icons of the emperor through the streets of Jerusalem, they felt that no Jew had the right to arouse the people to challenge Roman rule on religious grounds. As far as the procurators and the high priests were concerned, the line of demarcation between the realm of Caesar and the realm of God was a line that both God and the emperor had drawn.

It was not so easy, however, for the authorities to decide what to do about charismatic leaders who preached no violence and built no revolutionary organizations but rather urged the people to repent and to wait for the coming of God's kingdom. Were these charismatics harmless preachers or were they troublemakers? Were their teachings and visions goads to personal righteousness and therefore apolitical or even nonpolitical? Or were they goads to dissatisfaction and unhappiness with the world that was?

The prophetlike charismatics were preachers, not revolutionaries. They resembled the prophets of old. They did not call upon the people to rise up against Rome but to look to God, who had the power to perform miracles and move mountains. One such charismatic, Theudas, attracted vast crowds of credulous believers who followed him toward the Jordan River, anticipating that God would split the Jordan for him as certainly as it had been split for Joshua, only to have their hopes dashed when Roman soldiers apprehended Theudas and put him to death.

A similar fate befell another prophetlike redeemer—this one from Egypt. He was, according to Josephus, a charlatan who had gained the reputation of a prophet. This man appeared in the nation, collected a following of about thirty thousand, and led them by a circuitous route to the Mount of Olives. From there he proposed to force an entrance into Jerusalem and, after overpowering the Roman garrison, to set himself up as a tyrant of the people. His attack, however, was anticipated by the procurator, Felix, who went to meet him with the Roman infantry. The outcome of the ensuing engagement was that the Egyptian escaped with a few of his followers; most of his force was killed or taken prisoner; the remainder was dispersed and stealthily escaped to their several homes (*The Jewish War* II: 261–63).

Josephus chose Theudas and the Egyptian false prophet out of a seething prophetic brew. They were but two examples of the charismatics who flourished alongside the dagger-wielding Fourth Philosophers, also called the Sicarii. Josephus describes them as follows:

> A new species of banditti [sprang] up in Jerusalem, the so-called Sicarii, who committed murders in broad daylight in the heart of the city. The festivals were then special seasons when they would

> mingle with the crowd, carrying short daggers concealed under their clothing, with which they stabbed their enemies. Then, when they fell, the murderers joined in the cries of indignation and through this plausible behavior were never discovered. The first to be assassinated by them was Jonathan the high priest; after his death there were numerous daily murders. The panic created was more alarming than the calamity itself—everyone, as on the battlefield, hourly expecting death. Men kept watch at a distance on their enemies and would not trust even their friends when they approached. Yet even while their suspicions were aroused and they were on their guard, they fell—so swift were the conspirators and so crafty in eluding detection (*The Jewish War* II: 254–57).

Josephus gives us a feeling for the kind of chaos and anarchy that was prevalent and the kind of emotional and psychological disorientation that followed in its wake. He was not concerned with cataloguing an exhaustive list of charismatics. He selected a Theudas here, an Egyptian false prophet there as illustrative examples. He felt no need to name every prophetlike figure who stirred the people with visions of redemption. As a historian, he wished to convey the fact that suffering, distress, and disorientation had made the soil fertile for the resurrection of the spirit of prophecy, a spirit that had been so prominent in former days when suffering, distress, and disorientation had been dealt out by imperial powers. This resurrection of the prophetic spirit was for Josephus a frightening specter. Like his Pharisaic teachers, he believed that prophecy had come to an end with the death of Malachi. He looked on this outburst of prophetic fervor as fraudulent and dangerous—so much so, in fact, that he calls the perpetrators "deceivers and imposters . . . with purer hands but more impious intentions" and claims that they were no less responsible than the outright assassins for ruining the peace of Jerusalem.

Yet amid this cacophony of prophetic and charismatic voices, there were some that Josephus himself recognized as arising from sincere, righteous, and benign teachers, calling upon the people to turn their hearts and minds to God and repent of their sinful ways. He heard their calls for repentance not as calls for arms or even for miraculous deliverance but rather as calls for religious renewal, calls that no follower of the Scribes-Pharisees could gainsay.

One such charismatic was John the Baptist. Josephus's vignette of John is so essential to the thesis of this book that a portion of it is worthy of reiteration:

> *He was a good man and had exhorted the Jews to lead righteous lives, to practice justice toward their fellows and piety toward God.* . . . When others, too, joined the crowds about him *because they were aroused to the highest degree by his sermons, Herod* [the Tetrarch] *became alarmed. Eloquence that had so great an effect on mankind might lead to some form of sedition for it looked as if they would be guided by John in everything they did.*
>
> *Herod decided, therefore, that it would be much better to strike first and be rid of him before his work led to an uprising than to wait for an upheaval, get involved in a difficult situation, and see his mistake. . . . The verdict of the Jews was that the destruction visited upon Herod's army was a vindication of John, since God saw fit to inflict such a blow on Herod* (*Antiquities* XVIII: 116–19; emphasis mine).

Josephus's brief account is of striking value. It illuminates an obscure and murky landscape: the turf where religious claims to autonomy and Roman claims to sovereignty could not easily be differentiated. *There was no way to predict whether a pious charismatic's call for repentance would have unintended political consequences.* For most Jews, John was simply a preacher of righteousness whose teachings were free of political intent. John was calling for righteous lives, just actions, and pious commitments—not for a revolt against Rome. His baptism was no cleansing for battle against Caesar but the mark of a battle against sin already won. Nor was John dangling the prospect of miracles that would transform the earthly world but miracles that would transform the world within. Therefore, when the people learned that Herod Antipas had put John to death, they were appalled. Then when Herod's army was destroyed, they were gratified that the death of the goodly John had been avenged. Josephus is thus only summing up the attitude of a follower of the Scribes-Pharisees when he describes John as a good man who preached the righteous life so eloquently that his cruel death was worthy of being avenged by God himself.

Josephus's portrayal of John reveals that there could indeed be a charismatic teacher whose teachings were nonpolitical but could arouse fear in the hearts of the authorities, who were concerned only with the thought that the crowds gathering round him might get out of control and go on a rampage. Thus Herod the Tetrarch deemed it "better to strike first."

James, the brother of Jesus, was another apolitical preacher who was put to death by the high priest Ananus, to the dismay of those "strict observers of the Law," the Scribes-Pharisees. In his account, Josephus's sympathies are clearly with James and those "inhabitants of the city who were considered the most fair-minded and who were strict in observance of the law"—those who were offended by the high priest's high-handedness in convoking a sanhedrin in the absence of the procurator and in putting James to death (*Antiquities* XX:197–203).

Several issues here disturbed Josephus. First, there was the matter of jurisdiction, since Ananus had no right to convoke a sanhedrin on his own authority. The high priest was the political appointee of the procurator and, as such, could not carry out an execution without the express approval of the procurator. Hence when Ananus took the law into his own hands, it was recognized as a breach of his authority. The responsible leaders in Jerusalem immediately sent a message to Agrippa II, alerting him of Ananus's illegal actions. Others went directly to the procurator Albinus and informed him that Ananus had convened a sanhedrin without the procurator's consent. Outraged, Agrippa deposed Ananus from the high priesthood.

Second, although Ananus's action might have been prompted in part by his loyalty to the Sadducees in attempting to find a way to execute James, *the instrument that he used for this purpose—a sanhedrin—was a political, not a religious, body.* Since Ananus had no authority to convene a sanhedrin without the procurator's consent, such a council had no religious function. This is confirmed by the fact that the strict observers of the Law, the Scribes-Pharisees, were so aroused that they immediately took steps to have Ananus ousted. *It was not Ananus's displeasure with James's beliefs but his abuse of political authority that so outraged them. Ananus had used a political instrument, a sanhedrin, to rid himself of a religious dissident.* If Ananus had been allowed to get away with this breach of legality, he might at some future time have been tempted to use his political authority against the Scribes-Pharisees themselves.

Josephus's brief account of the reaction to the trial and execution of James reveals that religious dissidence was not viewed by the Scribes-Pharisees as sufficient justification for political repression. Political repression was allowable only to the degree that certain religious teachings might represent a clear and present political danger, a danger the Scribes-Pharisees obviously did not consider to have been represented by James's teachings. But it must be added that if there had been a clear and present danger, it still was not the high priest's place to make such a judgment on his own authority. The procurator alone had the ultimate responsibility for determining whether a dissident was or was not politically dangerous.

Josephus's account has another importance—an importance that scholars have tended to overlook. This is the only time Josephus mentions Jesus in a passage whose authenticity has never been challenged. Yet in this one passage, Josephus tosses out Jesus' name only parenthetically, so as to establish James's identity. *Nonetheless, by doing do, Josephus reveals that Jesus must have been well known to his readers.* In order to make clear to the reader the reason for the fuss and fury over James, Josephus merely points out that James was the brother of "Jesus called the Christ." Clearly no further explanation was necessary since every cultured Greek and Roman who might read Josephus's *Antiquities* would have known about the Christians. They thus would have understood immediately why James and his associates had been arrested, brought before a sanhedrin, and executed. After all, had that not happened to Jesus himself, the brother of James? *The single word* Christ *used by Josephus was thus sufficient to account for all that had happened.* It was not James who was on trial but his preaching that Jesus, the Christ, had risen from the dead—a claim that would especially arouse the wrath of a high priest who was a Sadducee. It would also help to explain why "the strict observers of the Law" were incensed. For though the Scribes-Pharisees may not have believed that Jesus was the Christ and had risen from the dead, they wanted no Sadducean high priest bringing the Pharisaic belief in resurrection into question. We need only recall how Paul provoked a clash between Pharisees and Sadducees when he was brought before a sanhedrin and cried out, "Brethren, I am a Pharisee, a son of Pharisees; with respect to the hope and the resurrection of the dead I am on trial" (Acts 23:6).

Josephus's testimony is revealing also because it makes clear that he did not believe James deserved death on the grounds of having preached the risen Christ. It makes clear, too, that "the strict observers of the Law" did not regard James's preachings as dangerous. Even though they themselves were loyal to Rome, they did not hesitate to let King Agrippa and Albinus know that they disapproved of what Ananus had done.

It is thus evident from Josephus's writing that there were influential Jews who drew a line between outright revolutionaries who called for the overthrow of Rome in God's name and charismatics who, like John the Baptist, called upon the people to repent or who, like James, the brother of Jesus, preached the risen Christ. They saw no danger to Rome in religious preachings that looked to God rather than to arms for salvation. Even though, in the case of James, these Jewish leaders rejected the claims that Jesus had risen from the dead, they still observed their doctrine of noninterference. God, not men, would be the ultimate arbiter. As Gamaliel, the Scribe-Pharisee, is reported to have said to the high priest's sanhedrin: "Keep away from these men and let them alone; for . . . if it is of God, you will not be able to overthrow them" (Acts 5:38–39). Surely, since the Sadducees daily preached outright rejection of the Pharisaic belief in the resurrection and the Scribes-Pharisees lifted no finger to harm them, then James, who acknowledged the Pharisaic belief in the resurrection each time he proclaimed Jesus as risen from the dead, should be left to God's judgment, not man's.

Josephus's testimony as to the state of affairs in Jesus' day is now spread before us. There were the Sadducees, Pharisees, and Essenes who adhered to the doctrine of the two realms and to the doctrine of live and let live. They had made their peace with Rome and with themselves. But alongside them were those revolutionaries who sought to overthrow Roman rule by force and those prophetlike charismatics who preached repentance and God's redemptive power. The reactions of these two groups to the harshness of Roman rule clashed with the passive acquiescence of the Sadducees, Scribes-Pharisees, and Essenes. The Fourth Philosophy could not insulate religious beliefs from political consequences, while the charismatics, advocating no violence, could delude themselves into thinking that as long as it was God, not men, who swept out Roman rule, the authorities might regard their preaching as devoid of political implications.

The Roman authorities, however, made no distinction. To them, revolutionaries and charismatics alike were outside the mosaic of Judaism. They all preached novel doctrines that set them apart from the Sadducees, Scribes-Pharisees, and Essenes. The charismatics were politically dangerous because their teachings and eloquence attracted crowds, and crowds were unpredictable and therefore dangerous. Charismatics, prophets, visionaries—all were potentially threatening and therefore better out of the way. The line between the two realms, insofar as the authorities were concerned, was clearly and sharply drawn. It was a line of demarcation that separated the mosaic of Judaism from those deviations that flowered from the seeds of violence that the emperor, the procurator, and the high priest had sown.

IN THE LIKENESS OF THE SON OF MAN

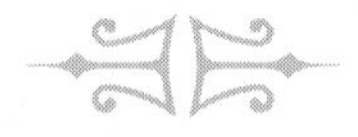

Amid the spiritual convulsions of those troubled times and amongst the prophetlike preachers and charismatics who were crying out the good news that God would soon redeem his people from bondage, we scan the writings of Josephus in vain for that charismatic of charismatics whom we would have anticipated finding there—a charismatic so compassionate, so loving, so eloquent, and so filled with the Spirit of God that his disciples would refuse to accept his death as real. But Josephus shares with us only the charismatic John the Baptist. Yet for all his charisma, John the Baptist failed to arouse in his disciples a love intense enough or a faith secure enough to evoke his death as but a prelude to life.

However overwhelmed with grief and however drawn to his person John's disciples may have been, they did not see him risen from the dead, even though the Scribes-Pharisees were daily preaching resurrection, just as they daily reaffirmed it when they recited the *Tefillah*, the prayer par excellence, as required by the twofold Law. John's charisma, however impressive and alluring, clearly lacked the power to sustain his life beyond the grave.

The sound, the fury, and the tumult of the times cry out for a charismatic of charismatics. Yet Josephus gives us no such unique individual. He readies us for a Jesus but gives us only John the Baptist. His fleeting allusion to Jesus as the brother of James fades away as he concentrates on James's fate, not Jesus' resurrection. Josephus's awareness that Jesus was called the Christ and that James must have preached him as risen from the dead remains unarticulated. For whatever reason, Josephus bespeaks John the Baptist, not Jesus called the Christ.

Josephus's silence stimulates us to try our own hand at painting a portrait of the missing charismatic of charismatics from the pigments of the age that Josephus has preserved in his palette. We ask ourselves: What manner of man would such a charismatic have been? What qualities must he have had to so endear himself to his disciples that even death itself did not have the power to pry them apart? What must his likeness have been to so entrance his followers that they were open-eyed to see his likeness as much alive after death as before? In a word: What qualities must this unique individual have possessed to make him an even more powerful and alluring charismatic than John?

For an individual to succeed in winning so devoted a following, he must have had fused within himself the wonder-working charisma of an Elijah, the visionary power of an Isaiah, the didactive persuasion of a Pharisaic sage. But he must have been more than a mere fusion of such guiding spirits. To outlive death itself, he would have had to *feel* the sufferings of the poor, *experience* the humiliation of the degraded, *sense* the loneliness of the outcast, *taste* the despair of the sinner, and *envelop* all who came within his shadow with his graciousness, compassion, and undemanding love.

He would, in addition, have had to exhibit all the commanding characteristics of the great prophets of action—Moses, Samuel,

Elijah, Elisha. Those prophets had been bold leaders, impressive wonder-workers, and freely accessible to the people at large. They had spoken simply, directly, and forcefully. They had acted fearlessly and decisively. Chosen by God to be his servants, none of them could have flinched or turned back. Whatever the hardship, whatever the pain, whatever the disappointment, their steadfast loyalty to God had never wavered.

Of all the prophets, Elijah would have had a special attraction for a charismatic of charismatics. Elijah, more than the other prophets of action, was of folklike hue. He had been a ruggedly austere man of God, yet his heart had overflowed with compassion. He had championed Naboth's cause when Ahab sought to confiscate the good man's vineyard. He had wrought miracles, bringing back to life the child of a good and simple woman who had offered him hospitality. He had stood up to King Ahab and heaped God's curses upon him, had challenged the prophets of Baal and brought them low. He had drifted about from place to place, a sojourner in his own land, and had sought refuge in a cave with only the still small voice of God to reassure and comfort him. It was he alone of all the prophets who had been whirled upward into heaven in a blazing chariot drawn by horses of fire (II Kings 2:11; cf. 2:10), and it was he alone whom God had assigned a special role in ushering in the great and terrible day of the Lord (Malachi 4:5).

Though for the charismatic of charismatics, Elijah would stand out most vividly, other prophets of action—Moses, Samuel, Elisha—would also have served as models. All had been charismatics; all had been fearless leaders; all had been endowed with wondrous power. "In troubled times such as these," he would wonder, "might not God raise up a prophet who would resemble a Moses, a Samuel, an Elijah, or an Elisha—one who would work wonders and lead the people out of their distress?"

Our charismatic of charismatics would have had, in addition to the great prophets of action, the grand visionary prophets to inspire him. Of these, Isaiah and Ezekiel were especially prominent. Isaiah had pictured a glorious end of days when the leopard would lie down with the lamb and swords would be beaten into ploughshares; when a shoot would come forth from the stump of Jesse and a branch would grow out of his roots, and the spirit of the Lord would rest upon him:

> The spirit of wisdom and understanding,
> the spirit of counsel and might,
> the spirit of knowledge and of the fear of the LORD.
>
> Isaiah 11:2

No other prophet etched so sharp an image of a messianic figure as did Isaiah—or so attractive a vignette of human fulfillment. For a charismatic of charismatics, the Anointed One of the stump of Jesse would be the Messiah, the model ruler, who

> shall not judge by what his eyes see
> or decide by what his ears hear;
> But with righteousness he shall judge the poor
> and decide with equity for the meek of the earth. . . .
> Righteousness shall be the girdle of his waist
> and faithfulness the girdle of his loins.
>
> Isaiah 11:3b–4, 5

The age the Messiah ushered in would be one in which

> the leopard shall lie down with the kid
> and the calf and the lion and the fatling together;
> and a little child shall lead them.
> The cow and the bear shall feed;
> their young shall lie down together;
> and the lion shall eat straw like the ox.
> The suckling child shall play over the hole of the asp,
> and the weaned child shall put his hand on the adder's den.
> They shall not hurt or destroy
> in all [God's] holy mountain;
> For the earth shall be full of the knowledge of the Lord
> as the waters cover the sea.
>
> Isaiah 11:6–9

For a charismatic of charismatics, this vision would have been a prophecy emanating from God and therefore bound to come to pass at the end of days.

This absolute trust in Isaiah's prophecy would have been reinforced by all the other prophets who had spun out visions of the end of days. The visions of Ezekiel with their picturings of the fury and tumult that would herald God's coming; the quickening of the dead; the restoring of the people of Israel to a renewed life under a beneficent shepherd of the house of David—all would have a powerful attraction. God had addressed Ezekiel also as Son of man, an elusive designation and one that could have aroused in a charismatic of charismatics the notion that *Son of man* might designate a person as being more than a prophet. Perhaps it was the name God would give his Anointed when the kingdom was finally at hand.

And then there was Malachi, who envisioned the end of days as coming on the heels of Elijah's return to earth, when he would "turn the hearts of fathers to their children and the hearts of children to their fathers" (Malachi 4:6).

A man able to fuse an Elijah with an Isaiah—behaving like the former and dreaming like the latter, being both a wonder-worker and a visionary—would indeed be fit for the role of charismatic of charismatics. He would mingle with the poor and lowly and revive their spirits with his spirit. He would stir them with hope and faith as he proclaimed that the kingdom of God was coming. He would look very much like a prophet of olden times, but he would also bear the likeness of the Son of man, the Anointed, the King-Messiah, ushering in the day of the Lord. He would have stamped on his countenance the image of an Elijah, the image of an Isaiah, and the fused image of the Son of man as both prophet and King-Messiah.

In addition to these, he would have fused within himself the model of a Scribe-Pharisee. This image would have been sui generis for it would have been that of a teacher who taught the Word of God, not that of a prophet who spoke the Word of God. Unlike the prophets, the Scribes-Pharisees never prefaced their teachings with "Thus saith Yahweh," even though what they taught—the *Halachah* (Oral Law) and the *Aggadah* (oral lore)—was deemed to be even more authoritative than that which had been uttered by even the greatest of prophets, Moses himself. The laws that God had commanded and that Moses had written down in the Pentateuch had been subordinated to the Oral Law of the Scribes-Pharisees, while the moral and ethical injunctions that God had revealed to Moses and to the prophets were themselves dependent upon the meaning assigned them by the Scribes-Pharisees.

The Scribe-Pharisee was thus cut from a very different cloth than the prophet of old. The Scribe-Pharisee was preeminently a teacher around whom disciples flocked and at whose feet they sat. Like the Stoic sage, the Scribe-Pharisee walked about with his disciples and freely discoursed on the Oral and Written Law and on the oral and written lore. Legal opinions mingled freely with reflections on God, Torah, Israel, and the struggle of the individual to subdue the power of sin so as to gain the bliss of the world to come. His discourses on Law and lore were punctuated with deftly chosen proof-texts from the Pentateuch, the Prophets, and the Hagiographa, giving their words the assured ring of divine authority by linking the Written with the Oral Law. The Scribe-Pharisee roamed Scripture, searching for verses, words, even letters that would become grist for his mill. Whatever meanings his own dicta required from these verses, words, and letters he elicited with flair and confidence.

Venerated and respected by the people at large, the Scribe-Pharisee taught with authority but an authority that was collective, not individual. It derived from being a bona fide teacher of the twofold Law—a teacher who, in Jesus' day, was a follower of either the school of Hillel or the school of Shammai. The time had not yet come when he was authorized to expound oral laws in his own name. This had to wait for the destruction of the Temple in A.D. 70. He was not yet called rabbi, *my teacher*, but only rab, *teacher*. As a teacher, he was an expositor of the twofold Law as agreed to by the scholar class as a whole or as expounded by the school with which he was affiliated.

But whether the Scribe-Pharisee was a follower of the school of Hillel or the school of Shammai, he was a devotee of the twofold Law and a firm believer in eternal life for the soul and resurrection for the body. He also was committed to the doctrine of the two realms and to the doctrine of live and let live. As such, he would be highly skeptical of would-be messiahs who dangled before the suffering masses the illusory hope of God's coming kingdom. The Scribe-Pharisee would be especially hostile toward any individual who claimed a singular authority derived from a special relationship to God and who looked upon himself as the Son of man or the King-Messiah. Such an individual would provoke the Scribe-Pharisee, who would challenge the would-be Son of man in debate, deride him before multitudes, even denounce him as Beelzebul's emissary. *But he would not drag him off to a* bet din (boulé) *of the Scribes-Pharisees, any more then he would drag there a Sadducee who derided belief in the twofold Law and resurrection.*

A charismatic of charismatics would nonetheless have been very much attracted to the leadership style of the Scribes-Pharisees. Indeed, at first glance, he would so resemble them that it would be difficult for the Scribes-Pharisees themselves to distinguish him from a teacher of the twofold Law. For like them, he would be a speaker, not a writer—an expositor of Law and lore who drove home his teachings with parables and paradigms and a sprinkling of illuminating proof-texts. Even the substance of his teachings would frequently echo those of the Scribes-Pharisees: He would proclaim God's Oneness; call on the people to love God with all their heart and being; urge his listeners to love their neighbors as themselves; acknowledge the legitimacy of Caesar's realm; and trumpet the good news of eternal life and resurrection. But when he spoke of a special relationship to God the Father, or flirted with the idea that he might be the Son of man, or exorcised demons, or displayed miraculous powers of healing, or spoke of God's kingdom as being at hand, or edged toward looking upon himself as the King-Messiah, his resemblance to a Scribe-Pharisee would fade away. The Scribes-Pharisees would reject any seeming likeness of the charismatic of charismatics to a Pharisaic sage. They would call so aberrant a teacher to task for leading the people astray with his delusions and would denounce his claims as spurious.

A charismatic of charismatics would thus appear to be an amalgam of three venerated leadership types: the prophet of action, the prophet of vision, and the Scribe-Pharisee. Depending upon what he was teaching or doing at any given moment and depending upon who was listening to him, he would seem to be now an Elijah, now an Isaiah, now a Scribe-Pharisee. But the decisive point would not be the likenesses—however powerful and alluring they might be—but the goodness, the compassion, the gentleness of soul, which reached out with caring love to the lowly, the disheartened, the dispirited. Only qualities such as these could bind those whom he touched with cords of love and faith, cords so taut that even death could not relax them. It was not the fusing of an Elijah, an Isaiah, and a Scribe-Pharisee into his person—these alone would not have rendered him deathless; perhaps even John the Baptist may have effected such a fusion—but his healing and loving spirit, which had the power to restore souls to life.

If such a charismatic had taught and preached during the years when Pontius Pilate was procurator and Caiaphas was high priest, what would his fate have been? None other, we can be sure, than the fate that had overtaken John the Baptist. If such a charismatic were believed to be an Elijah when he healed the sick, raised the dead, and cast forth demons, his wonder-working would have attracted crowds—and crowds, as we know, were dangerous and could get out of hand. If he seemed to be a visionary and, like Isaiah, proclaimed that the kingdom of God was near at hand, his high hopes would have attracted crowds—and crowds, as we know, were dangerous and could get out of hand. If he bore a likeness to the Son of man, the King-Messiah, his likeness would have attracted crowds—and crowds, as we know, were dangerous and could get out of hand. And if his compassion and love reached and lifted up the wretched, gave hope to the outcast and reassurance to the faint of heart, such compassion and love would have attracted crowds—and crowds, as we know, were dangerous and could get out of hand.

Crowds were dangerous indeed! So dangerous, in fact, that Herod the Tetrarch had put John the Baptist to death—not because John urged the people to repent, live pious lives, and undergo baptism, but only because his eloquence attracted crowds and crowds were unpredictable and prone to violence. Ever since the young firebrands had torn down the Roman eagle in God's name, violence had become a normal response to Roman provocation. Even the presence of Roman legionnaires in the Temple precincts could not deter crowds from going berserk.

What chance for survival would a charismatic of charismatics have—this man of eloquence, wonder-works, religious fervor, fevered fantasies, messianic pretensions, and sheer charisma—if his person attracted crowds in Jerusalem, where Pontius Pilate and his high priest Caiaphas quaked at every rustle of discontent and every wisp of dissidence? No chance at all! For was this not the same Pilate who had dared to parade the icons of the emperor through the city? Was this not the same Pilate who had dressed his soldiers in civilian garb to mingle with the crowds so as to provoke them to riot and give him a pretext to cut them down? And was not Caiaphas, whose piercing eyes and keen ears had kept him in office throughout Pilate's procuratorship, the high priest?

With such a pair, can there be any doubt that they would have taken even fewer chances than had Herod the Tetrarch were a charismatic of charismatics to appear in Jerusalem attracting crowds? Would Pontius Pilate or Caiaphas care a fig for what the man taught or preached? And if the charismatic were attracting crowds because it seemed to many that he was the Son of man, the King-Messiah about to usher in the kingdom of God, would they not pounce on him swiftly and hasten him to the cross, the ultimate Roman deterrent for keeping revolutionaries and would-be messiahs at bay? For Pontius Pilate and Caiaphas, danger to Rome lurked as much behind the visions of an Isaiah, the prophecies of an Ezekiel, the mantle of an Elijah, or the likeness of the Son of man as behind the sheathed dagger of a Judas of Galilee.

A charismatic of charismatics would thus have had no chance of survival at all. To the degree that he proved himself to be such a charismatic through his healing of the sick, his casting out of demons, his raising of the dead, his arousing of hopes for the coming of God's kingdom—to that degree would he attract crowds. And if this charismatic of charismatics actually tested his faith and that of his followers by parading through Jerusalem among crowds who were chanting "The Messiah, the Son of man is among us—Hosanna in the highest" and by appearing in the Temple precincts as a champion of piety and rectitude, Caiaphas would have been provoked to decisive action, lest his failure to act be mistaken as a sign of either permissiveness or fear. With his high priestly office dangling on his detection of sparks of violence before they burst into flames, Caiaphas would lose no time in silencing so ominous a threat to law and order.

Events then would have occurred with blurring rapidity. Caiaphas would have had the charismatic of charismatics brought before his privy council, a sanhedrin of the high priest, and would have charged him with undermining Roman authority by his teachings, his preachings, and his actions. For he had taught and preached that the kingdom of God was near at hand, a kingdom that, were it to come, would displace the kingdom of Rome. By creating the impression that he might be the Son of man, the King-

Messiah who would usher in God's kingdom, he had, in fact, sought to reign in Caesar's stead. And by stirring up the crowds, parading as he did through Jerusalem and causing a commotion in the precincts of the Temple, he had readied the people for riotous behavior. His teachings, preachings, and actions were bound to sway the loyalties of the Jews: God disapproved of the emperor, God disapproved of the procurator, and God disapproved of the procurator-appointed high priest. The fact that the charismatic of charismatics had taught no violence, had preached no revolution, and had lifted up no arms against Rome's authority would have been utterly irrelevant. The high priest Caiaphas and the procurator Pontius Pilate cared not a whit how or by whom the kingdom of God would be ushered in but only that the Roman emperor and his instruments would not reign over it.

With charges such as these flung at him in the presence of Caiaphas's hand-chosen privy councillors, the fate of the charismatic would be sealed. He had undermined law and order by his words and deeds. He had sowed the seeds of mass demonstrations and contagious violence. These alone were the issues. *Neither his religious teachings nor his beliefs could have been on trial, only their potential political consequences, for the sanhedrin was the high priest's council, which had no function other than to advise the high priest on political matters.* All those who sat on this sanhedrin were committed to the doctrine of the two realms—a doctrine to which Sadducees and Pharisees and Essenes adhered. *As a body appointed and convened by a religious illegitimate, the sanhedrin of the high priest had no authority over religious matters.* Sadducees could sit beside Pharisees only as individuals concerned with preserving the compact with Rome, a compact that guaranteed religious autonomy to the Jews as long as the Jews recognized Roman sovereignty. The high priest's sanhedrin thus could not have been a *bet din* (*boulé*) for the issues to be dealt with were political issues, not religious ones.

These, then, were the questions they would have asked themselves: Were the man's charisma and teachings attracting crowds? What were the chances that the people might go berserk and provoke the procurator into ordering out the troops? Even though the charismatic himself was a man of peace, not of violence; a visionary, not a revolutionary; a gentle and compassionate healer and teacher, not a rabble-rouser, he could release a tempest of violence.

Empathy for the charismatic's plight would have been counterbalanced by empathy for the hundreds, if not thousands, who might be butchered by the Roman soldiers if the crowds misheard, misunderstood, or brushed aside the pleas of the charismatic that violence was not what he had meant at all—that God, not the violence of men, would usher in his kingdom.

The outcome of such a trial would thus have been cut-and-dried. The high priest, as the eyes and ears of the procurator, was not a free agent. The members of the council, the sanhedrin that he convoked, were likewise not free agents. The charismatic had attracted crowds with his preachings, his wonder-workings, and his charisma. As such, he was potentially dangerous. There could be few grounds for hesitancy or mitigation. *If the charismatic either claimed to be or was believed to be the Son of man, the Messiah, the King of the Jews, and if he was preaching the imminent coming of the kingdom of God, which of necessity would displace the kingdom of Rome, then the case was open and shut.* There was no recourse for the high priest but to advise the procurator that the charismatic of charismatics was in contempt of the emperor and a potential source of disruption and violence, however couched his teachings might be in prophetic imagery and however much he might emphasize that the kingdom of God was to be brought in by God, not man.

The high priest and the sanhedrin would thus report to the procurator the simple facts: Here is a charismatic of charismatics who attracted crowds; who set off a disturbance in the Temple area, thronged at festival time with highly excitable pilgrims; who was acclaimed as the Messiah, the King of the Jews, as he walked through the streets of Jerusalem; and who called upon the people to prepare themselves for the coming of God's kingdom—not at some distant time in the future, as the Scribes-Pharisees taught, but at any moment, in the twinkling of an eye.

It would then be up to the procurator to make a final decision as to whether he concurred with the facts and the judgment: Was the charismatic sufficiently dangerous to be crucified as a warning to other charismatics that their religious teachings would be judged by the political consequences that might follow in their wake? *Crucifixion awaited both the revolutionary and charismatic.* Pontius Pilate, a procurator notorious for his high-handedness and ruthlessness, would have made short shrift of a case like this. A rebel against

Rome was a rebel against Rome, however much he cloaked his rebellion in talk of God. Such a rebel belonged on the cross—not in the hills of Galilee, or in the streets of Jerusalem, or in the precincts of the Temple. His agony, his helplessness, and his failure would discourage other charismatics from dreaming dangerous dreams. It would discourage the people at large from following dreamlike images of the Son of man, the would-be king-messiahs, the deluded weavers of a fantasy kingdom of God that would never come. For Pontius Pilate, a charismatic served up to him by his loyal and competent Caiaphas would have been a welcome opportunity for a display of Caesar's might.

But would not the teaching and preaching of the charismatic of charismatics have been so religiously provocative as to have aroused the anger of the Scribes-Pharisees? Would not the Scribes-Pharisees have been affronted by his wonder-working, his casting out of demons, his cavalier disregard for the Traditions of the Elders, his posturing as the Son of man and the Messiah? And would they not have brought him before a *bet din* (*boulé*) on the charge of blasphemy or its equivalent? The answer to these questions is no! *For just as the Scribes-Pharisees adhered to the doctrine of the two realms, so, too, did they adhere to the doctrine of live and let live.* They did not haul Sadducees before their *bet din* (*boulé*) even though the Sadducees rejected the twofold Law. They did not prohibit a Sadducean high priest from carrying out his duties in the Temple, however heretical in their sight he might have been, as long as he did not deviate from the procedures set down by the Scribes-Pharisees. They would surely challenge the claims of a charismatic: They would mock and ridicule him; pummel him with invectives; even pray for his undoing—but that was as far as they could go. Their legal jurisdiction no more extended to a charismatic than it did to Caiaphas, a Sadducee, who looked upon the Oral Law as a fraud, the Scribes-Pharisees as blasphemous usurpers, and reward and punishment beyond the grave as the cruelest illusion of all.

The fate of charismatics was thus sealed by a process that began with a trial before the high priest and his sanhedrin and ended with the procurator's sentence of death by crucifixion—a process that was political throughout in its intent and purpose. His crime would have been lèse-majesté—proclaimed to all by the *titulus* above the cross, mocking his pretension to be the King of the Jews. The charismatic had crossed the line that separated the turf of Caesar from the turf of God. He had crossed over into that no-man's-land where every life was forfeit. He may have been naive, but his political innocence would not spare him. There was a war being waged daily in Galilee, in the streets of Jerusalem, and in the Temple courts. Thousands already had been killed, maimed, burned, and crucified. Thousands more were destined to share the same fate. The people had become ungovernable. From day to day, Pontius Pilate did not know whether he would be procurator on the morrow. Caiaphas knew not at nightfall whether, when morning dawned, he would be high priest. One provocative act, one unguarded moment, one still small voice proclaiming the kingdom of God and the people could go wild with a frenzy that would not calm itself until the troops had butchered Jews by the hundreds, if not thousands. With their fate precariously dangling on the edge of each decision, Pontius Pilate and Caiaphas were hardly likely to spare a charismatic of charismatics whose innocence and naiveté had allowed him to stumble over the line that separated God's turf from Caesar's.

The cross would have been the fate that awaited a charismatic of charismatics, but it would not necessarily have been his destiny. For if his disciples had come to believe that he was indeed the Son of man and if he had bound them tightly to his person by his charisma, then there was every likelihood that their belief in him would have remained unshaken even though they heard him gasp with his last breath "God, why hast thou forsaken me?"—every likelihood—for at the very core of his teaching would have been his sturdy faith in the good news of the Scribes-Pharisees that the souls of the righteous soar up to God the Father, where they await the day of resurrection. Nothing could have been more certain to him than this promise. Resurrection, far from being impossible, was inevitable. And if inevitable, how could it be denied by his disciples if they saw their Teacher risen from the dead? For them, this would be the proof that he must be the Son of man, the King-Messiah. This was a happening that would confute the Scribes-Pharisees: The charismatic of charismatics must be the Messiah because he had risen from the dead.

Stunned, bewildered, disoriented, disbelieving the sight of their beloved Teacher crucified, would not the faithful have seen what the faithless could not—that their Master, their Teacher, their Lord was as alive as he ever had been when he had preached among them? And would they not exultantly then have shouted out the good news from the rooftops, proclaimed throughout the land that the Christ had risen from the dead, that he soon would be seen coming, with the kingdom of God following in his wake? And would not their faith in what they had seen be so strong that they would have been able to withstand the challenge and mockery of the nonseers? And would it not have been so tenacious that they would even be willing to face the beasts at Ephesus with joy?

And would not, then, the difference between a charismatic of charismatics such as this man and a charismatic such as John the Baptist lie precisely in this: that while the charismatic's life would have ended in death, the death of the charismatic of charismatics would have ended in Life?

JESUS, KING OF THE JEWS

We have drawn a portrait of a charismatic of charismatics whose life would have ended in Life. We have drawn it from Josephus's writings; Josephus himself did not draw it for us. It is a portrait of a charismatic who would have lived and died and been seen as resurrected. Given the time, the place, the situation, and the mind-set, this portrait is as real as life itself.

But there were those who painted portraits of a charismatic of charismatics who had actually lived—portraits that they believed expressed the very likeness of a remarkable person who had lived, died, and been seen as resurrected while Pontius Pilate was procurator and while Caiaphas was high priest. That charismatic of charismatics whose portrait they painted was Jesus the Messiah, the Son of man, the resurrected one. Yet though those portraits describe the same man, they so differ from one another as to put us at a loss to know which portrait bears the greatest likeness.

We thus find ourselves in a quandary. On the one hand, we have drawn a portrait from Josephus of a charismatic of charismatics who might have lived, died, and been seen as resurrected. On the other hand, we have in the Four Gospels of Mark, Matthew, Luke, and John portraits of Jesus drawn from real life preserved. Yet these portraits are so at variance that we cannot be certain which is the most lifelike. Perhaps we can extricate ourselves from our dilemma by placing the portrait of the charismatic of charismatics that we have drawn next to the portraits of Jesus as painted in the Gospels.

Let us look first at the portrait of Jesus drawn in the Gospel of John, since that one bears the least resemblance to the one we have drawn. We find that, indeed, there is hardly any resemblance at all. John's portrait of Jesus is one we could not have imagined from the writings of Josephus. It is a portrait that presupposes a different time, a different space, and a different mind-set. It is a portrait appropriate for a historical setting where the Christian communities are made up entirely of Gentiles and are spread throughout the cities of the Roman world. These Christians are far more interested in the Son of God, whose destiny was the cross and resurrection, than in the Son of man, who had preached the coming of God's kingdom to redeem the household of Israel. John's Gospel sees Jesus almost exclusively in the light of the resurrection rather than in the light of history. What Jesus actually said and did while he was alive was significant, in John's view, only to the degree that it reflected or illuminated Christ's divine (not human) destiny. For John, Jesus is the Divine Light whose humanity refracts his divinity. He is no mere mortal, a simple charismatic of charismatics whose humanity stirs the hearts and souls of those he touches and whose teaching arouses within them the hope for the coming of God's kingdom.

This divine role is evident the moment we open the Gospel of John. The Evangelist does not begin with a prophetic proclamation, as does Mark; or with a genealogy, as does Matthew; or with an assurance that his Gospel can be relied upon as accurately portraying Jesus' words and deeds, as does Luke. Instead, John begins with an outright declaration that God and the Logos, the Word of God, are one and the same and that they are the source of Light and Life (1:1–4). John the Baptist, according to the Evangelist, came not to announce that someone greater than he was to be the Redeemer but to bear witness to the Divine Light that was about to come into the world (1:19ff). Though John portrays the Christ as the Divine Light, he is not recognized as such by the Jews to whom he first appears. He is, however, recognized as the Divine Light by the Gentiles (1:11–12).

Jesus' own people were thus blind to the Divine Light. They were so blind that they hounded him and conspired with the authorities to have him crucified. The Gentiles, not the Jews, are thus the true seed of Abraham. Jesus' kinsmen in the flesh had shown themselves to be no kinsmen in the Spirit. The Gentiles alone proved worthy of being the people of God. The Gospel of John thus elevates Jesus out of his historical setting onto a timeless plane. Whereas the Synoptic Gospels are enigmatic as to the purpose of Jesus' ultimate fate, the Gospel of John is certain that he came to be crucified and to be resurrected.

From the very beginning of the Gospel of John, Christ's earthly sojourn is a trajectory from light to Light, from life to Life, and from father to Father. The Christ passes through this world in a body of flesh and blood only in order that his divinity may shine forth—first through his life, then through his "death" and resurrection. All who saw the Light shining through his life and were enlightened by it were destined to enjoy eternal life. The crucifixion was thus inexorable and necessary. It was something Jesus anticipated and welcomed. It was an event that revealed the blindness of the Jews who sought his crucifixion; an event that exposed their malevolence; an event that demonstrated that they were unworthy of remaining the people of God—an unworthiness they revealed when they refused to see Jesus risen from the dead. By contrast, the Gentiles demonstrated their worthiness to replace the Jews as the people of God when they saw Jesus risen from the dead and when they believed what they saw.

It is not surprising, therefore, that when we read the Gospel of

John, we see a Jesus above time, above place, above constraining frameworks. John sets Jesus off from the Jews as though Jesus himself had been a Gentile. He seems unaware that not all Jews were Pharisees and overlooks Jesus' controversies with the Pharisees regarding the binding character of the Traditions of the Elders. Likewise, John's failure to refer to the Scribes, mentioning only the Pharisees, illuminates how little John seems to know or care about the historical setting in which Jesus preached. So, too, John's use of the term *Passover* to refer to the entire festival is at odds with the Synoptics' distinction between Passover, which refers only to the first day of the festival, and Feast of Unleavened Bread, which in Jesus' day was the designation for the remaining days of the festival. John's portrait of Jesus thus bears little resemblance to our portrait drawn from Josephus—that of a charismatic of charismatics emerging out of the matrix of time, structure, process, and causality.

Not so with the Synoptic Gospels. The portraits of Jesus found in the Gospels of Mark, Matthew, and Luke portray a Jesus who, however much he may have been "out of this world," was part and parcel of it as well. He is pictured as a prophetlike figure, a charismatic of charismatics, the Son of man who enjoys a special relationship to God the Father. In Mark, we are told that there were some people who believed that Jesus was John the Baptist resurrected and hence endowed with miraculous powers; there were others who believed him to be Elijah; there were still others who believed that he was a prophet like the prophets of old—all images evoking charismatics whom God had endowed with supernatural powers (6:14–16). And even when Jesus is transfigured, he is pictured as being with Elijah and Moses as one who, like them, had a special relationship with God (Matthew 17:3; Mark 9:4; Luke 9:30). Here Jesus is humanized, personalized, and historicized. Jesus becomes credible because he is reminiscent of an Elijah and a Moses. He is not a divine being with no biblical prototype.

The portraits in the Synoptic Gospels, with all their differences in shading and nuance, stand out in sharp contrast to John's portrait of Jesus. There are clearly discernible features that bear a striking resemblance to the charismatic of charismatics whom we have drawn from Josephus; for the words and deeds of our projected charismatic of charismatics, like those of Jesus, would have evoked images of John the Baptist, Elijah, Moses, and the prophets of old in the minds of those who listened to Jesus and observed his wonder-working powers. So, too, Jesus' journey from life to Life as traced in the Synoptic Gospels is the very trajectory that our projected charismatic of charismatics would have taken—the path of a person of flesh and blood in whom the Spirit of God dwelled and who became thereby worthy of resurrection.

This human life of Jesus as delineated in the Synoptic Gospels sets him firmly in the historical matrix of the times. John the Baptist, a real charismatic, is held up as a precursor and a prototype. He is the same good man in the Synoptics as in Josephus. He is the voice crying in the wilderness, preaching a baptism of repentance and proclaiming the coming of God's kingdom—a kingdom not to be ushered in by him but by one who is to come after him, one more blessed and more worthy than he. Whereas John baptized with water, he who is to come will baptize with the Holy Spirit (Mark 1:2–4, 7–8; cf. Matthew 3:2, 11–12; Luke 3:4–6, 15–18). Mark and the other Synoptic Gospel writers are telling their readers that while John the Baptist was only a charismatic, Jesus was a charismatic of charismatics.

As such, Jesus trudges a road of his own making. Though frequenting the synagogue, he does not acknowledge any limitations on his teachings: He speaks out with a *singular* authority, an authority that arouses astonishment because it is so unlike the authority of the Scribes-Pharisees, which was collective, not individual. As the Son of man, Jesus does not hesitate to pronounce God's forgiveness of the sins of a paralytic, even though this divinelike act arouses the Scribes, who insist that God alone has the power to forgive sins. They charge Jesus with blasphemy, to which Jesus replies that, as the Son of man, he does have that authority (Matthew 9:1–8; Mark 2:1–12; Luke 5:17–26).

Jesus is no less defiant when he eats with sinners and tax collectors, even though the Scribes-Pharisees disapprove. When Jesus explains that he has come to call only sinners, not the righteous, they become even more infuriated since his words bespeak a rejection of their authority (Matthew 9:9–13; Mark 2:13–17; Luke 5:27–32). Nor can the Scribes-Pharisees submit to Jesus' right to take the Law into his own hands when he allows his disciples to pluck ears of grain on the Sabbath (Matthew 12:1–8; Mark 2:23–28; Luke 6:1–5); or when he shrugs off their eating with unwashed hands (Matthew 15:1–20; Mark 7:1-23); or when he himself heals a man's withered arm on the Sabbath (Matthew 12:9–14; Mark 3:1–6; Luke 6:6–11). Brushing aside the Traditions of the Elders as man-made, not God-made, he denounces his accusers as hypocrites (Mark 7:8–13; cf. Matthew 15:3–9).

Confronted with such behavior, the Scribes-Pharisees were at a loss as to what manner of man this was who healed the sick and spoke so assuredly of the kingdom of God that was about to come. Was he a teacher? (Mark 9:38) Was he a prophet, like one of the prophets of old? Elijah? Or even Moses, perhaps? Was he John, resurrected from the dead? (Matthew 14:1–2; Mark 6:14–16; Luke 9:7–9) Was he the Son of man? Was he the Messiah who would restore the kingdom of father David? (Mark 11:9–10; cf. Matthew 21:9; Luke 12:38) And what of his impressive powers and charisma—were they of God, or were they of Beelzebul, the Prince of Demons? (Matthew 12:22–24; Mark 3:19–22; Luke 11:14–16)

Sitting in Moses' seat, the Pharisees were forced to take a stand. Jesus, they concluded, was no simple replica of John the Baptist. He was a messianic pretender and, as such, must be exposed as a fraud. This the Scribes-Pharisees tried to do by using their authority to undermine his claims. If Jesus exorcised demons, then he must be Beelzebul's instrument (Matthew 12:24; Mark 3:22; Luke 11:15). If he healed on the Sabbath day, he must be a violator of the Law (Matthew 12:10; Mark 3:2; Luke 6:7). If he allowed his disciples to eat with unwashed hands (Matthew 15:2; Mark 7:5) or to pluck ears of grain on the Sabbath (Matthew 12:2; Mark 2:24; Luke 6:2), he was mocking the Traditions of the Elders. If he forgave sins, he was a blasphemer (Matthew 9:2–3; Mark 2:5–7; Luke 5:20–21). If he seemed to be a prophet, where were his signs? (Matthew 12:38) If he were the Anointed, where was Elijah? (Matthew 17:10; Mark 9:11) If he were the Messiah, son of David, where was his genealogy? (Matthew 22:41–42; Mark 12:35; Luke 20:41) If he preached that the kingdom of God was coming, should the tribute to Caesar be paid or not? (Matthew 22:17; Mark 12:14; Luke 20:22)

It is one thing, however, to try to expose Jesus as a fraud; it is quite another to succeed. Jesus proves to be nimble-minded. He returns barb for barb. Beelzebul, the Prince of Demons, would scarcely destroy his own house (Matthew 12:25–26; Mark 3:23–26; Luke 11:17–18). The Son of man, he claims with a proof-text on hand, need not be a descendant of David (Matthew 22:41–45; Mark 12:36–37; Luke 20:42–44). As for the payment of tribute, he, *echoing the Scribes-Pharisees*, insists that one must render unto Caesar what is Caesar's and unto God what is God's (Matthew 22:21; Mark 12:17; Luke 20:25).

The Scribes-Pharisees again and again find themselves mystified. On occasion, Jesus appears to be an exemplary teacher, adroitly and deftly countering the Sadducees who poke fun at the belief in resurrection (Matthew 22:23–33; Mark 12:18–27; Luke 20:27–40). And he draws the approval of a Scribe-Pharisee by affirming that "Hear, O Israel: The Lord is our God, the Lord is One; and you shall love the Lord your God with all your heart, and with all your soul, and with all your mind, and with all your strength" is the heart of the Law, while loving one's neighbor as oneself runs a close second (Mark 12:28–34; cf. Matthew 22:34–40; Luke 10:25–28).

The Scribes-Pharisees thus had no easy time challenging Jesus. He seemed at times to be one of them, but again he seemed not to be one of them at all. He adhered to the core teachings of the Scribes-Pharisees yet flaunted their authority by claiming a special relationship to God and by making light of the Traditions of the Elders. Thus when Jesus sought to compare his authority to that of John the Baptist, the Scribes-Pharisees, though left speechless, would have none of it (Mark 11:27–33). John may indeed have been a charismatic like Jesus, but he had kept his charisma within acceptable bounds. John had called for repentance as did the Scribes-Pharisees—only more so. He had called for justice as did the Scribes-Pharisees—only more so. John's call to baptism as a sign of the inner purification of the soul was a call the Scribes-Pharisees could applaud. Though John had proclaimed that the kingdom of God was at hand, he had not embarrassed the Scribes-Pharisees as had Jesus, with his allusions to being the Son of man or the King-Messiah.

Yet John's benign teachings had not spared him a tragic fate. His eloquence had attracted crowds, and crowds were dangerous. The political authorities took no chances. They had put him to death, though Josephus looked upon John as a good and righteous man. Jesus' teachings would thus be even more threatening. They were far more disruptive than any advanced by John. For Jesus, unlike John, had provoked the Scribes-Pharisees by flaunting his special relationship to God and by persisting in his ways: His healings continued; his exorcisms continued; his sitting with sinners continued; his preaching of the coming kingdom of God continued. And crowds gathered round him to hear, to see, to hope; and they struck fear in the heart of Caiaphas.

The more demons Jesus exorcised, the more mustard seeds he spread abroad, the more crowds he drew, the more irresistible his claims to be the Son of man, the King-Messiah, the Redeemer of Israel, the more the authorities feared an incident in the crowded streets of Jerusalem. They especially feared a demonstration on the Temple Mount as tens of thousands of Jews crowded into Jerusalem—perhaps a more violent demonstration than that described in the Gospels when Jesus overthrew the tables of the money changers and cried out that the Temple had become a den of robbers.The crowds were feared no less when they shouted in the streets "Hosanna! Blessed is he who comes in the name of the Lord! Blessed is the kingdom of our father David that is coming! Hosanna in the highest!" (Mark 11:9–10)

It would make no difference to the political authorities whether such incidents were sparked by religious zeal or by political expectations, or whether these incidents were spontaneous or orchestrated outbursts. *Indeed, it mattered not who said what, or what sparked whom, or who sparked what, or what the political motivation of the sparker happened to be. Even if Jesus had pleaded for measured calm by calling out "This is not what I meant at all, not at all," it would have made no difference to the authorities.* What mattered were the consequences for high priest and procurator if the crowds had gone wild, shouting "The kingdom of God is at hand, and Jesus is our King." The coming of God's kingdom would, in fact, have been even more frightening to Pontius Pilate and Caiaphas than a mere human kingdom since God's kingdom could be blocked by no earthly power, however exalted and mighty.

The Synoptic Gospels portray Caiaphas and Pontius Pilate as

doing exactly what we would have expected them to do, knowing as we do the tragic fate of John the Baptist. We are not surprised, therefore, to learn that Caiaphas moved against Jesus as quietly as he could, lest angry crowds gather, and had him brought, as we would have expected, before the high priest's sanhedrin of privy councillors, handpicked for their loyalty to the doctrine of two realms and for their sense of concern about a savage Roman response to any riotous behavior of the crowds, irrespective of its source (Matthew 26:3–5, 57–68).

The followers of Jesus thus told it as it had actually happened. *Jesus was brought before the only body that had jurisdiction over those who were charged with breaking or endangering the peace: the high priest's sanhedrin, convoked by him and presided over by him. Despite the hostility they may have harbored for the Scribes-Pharisees, the disciples of Jesus did not report that Jesus had been brought before a* bet din (boulé), *presided over by a teacher of the twofold Law, to be charged with a violation of God's Law. They did not so report because in Jesus' day, all Jews living in Judea and Galilee knew that a charismatic would never be brought before a religious body to stand trial for his life, however deviant his religious teachings.*

The Synoptic Gospels' accounts are thus historically credible since they exonerate the *bet din* (*boulé*) from any role in the trial and crucifixion of Jesus. They bear true witness to the imperial system and its jurisdiction over political issues; to the doctrine of the two realms espoused by the Scribes-Pharisees with respect to the political and religious realms; and to the doctrine of live and let live with respect to divergent forms of Judaism.

The Gospels likewise confirm our expectations when they tell us that Jesus was charged with the crime of being the Son of man, the Messiah, the King of the Jews. *For the issue was not a religious issue even though these images were grounded in the Hebrew Scriptures.* The prophets had envisioned an end of days when all pain and suffering and anguish—even death itself—would be stilled. Isaiah had visualized a King-Messiah, sprung from the stump of Jesse, who would reign in glory. Ezekiel had been addressed by God as the Son of man.

And here lies the tragedy of it all: These images rooted in Scriptures did indeed have political implications. God's kingdom in was

Rome's kingdom out! There was no way Jesus' preaching of God's kingdom could be disentangled from politics. *The high priest, the high priest's sanhedrin, and the procurator—all were bound to look upon Jesus' teachings as politically dangerous, however free they were of overt political intent.* Jesus' preaching of the coming of God's kingdom was treasonous in their eyes as long as that kingdom had no place for the Roman emperor, his procurator, and his procurator-appointed high priest. Only if Jesus were in truth the Son of man and the King-Messiah could the prophetic promise of a Messianic Age be acknowledged as having been fulfilled in him. But this was dependent on his actually bringing in the kingdom despite all human efforts to block it. In a word, Jesus would need to prove his claim by living, not by dying.

The Synoptic Gospels thus confirm that Jesus suffered the fate that would have befallen the charismatic of charismatics we have drawn from Josephus. For the Gospels tell us that Jesus was brought before Caiaphas, an appointee of the procurator, and before the high priest's sanhedrin—not before a *bet din* (*boulé*) of the Scribes-Pharisees—and charged with having claimed to be the Messiah, the King of the Jews. But though the Gospels clearly testify that Jesus was tried by a political body, the followers of Jesus may have believed that he had been tried on religious grounds. *For in their eyes, Jesus was the Son of man, God's Anointed*—a divinely not a humanly crowned King. He was necessarily a fulfillment of God's promise. He was thus ipso facto a religious, not a political, figure.

The high priest and his sanhedrin, however, had no such belief. For them, Jesus was deluded and his followers were deluded. He was just another would-be messiah whose naive illusions could spark an uprising. It is not surprising, therefore, that Jesus' disciples, who believed him to be the Christ, would attribute religious motives to the high priest and his sanhedrin since for the disciples, Jesus was exclusively a religious instrument of God, not a political figure. No wonder, then, that the Gospels blur the distinction between the political and the religious motivations, of which the high priest and his sanhedrin were always conscious.

This same blurring envelopes Pontius Pilate. Here, too, the Gospels fulfill our expectations. Jesus, like any charismatic, would have been brought before the procurator once the high priest and his sanhedrin were convinced that he was a threat to law and order. The procurator, for his part, would ask only one question: Are you the King of the Jews? And he would not be diverted by some Delphic answer such as "You have said so" (Matthew 27:11; Mark 15:2; Luke 23:3). For Pontius Pilate, the judgment of his trusted high priest Caiaphas would have been enough.

But Pontius Pilate, as we know from Josephus, had his own political agenda. As one who was given to provoking Jews with wily stratagems, Pilate was not beyond using a politically naive charismatic, one who claimed to be their King, to entrap the Jews. By giving the crowds a choice between the release of a revolutionary[3] such as Barabbas, who made no claim to being King of the Jews, and a charismatic who did make such a claim, Pilate was, in effect, compelling the crowd to choose the revolutionary. They would fear to choose the other lest Pilate loose his soldiery on them for acknowledging a king other than Caesar (Matthew 27:15–23; Mark 15:6–15; Luke 23:18–25).

Pontius Pilate's strategy, however, could hardly have been discerned by the politically naive followers of Jesus. All they could see and comprehend was that the crowds, egged on by the priests, were calling for Barabbas. Little wonder that *their* anger would be directed against the other Jews rather than against Pontius Pilate, who was taunting the crowd to name Jesus as their king. When we read of this incident in the light of our knowledge of Pilate's provocative tricks, we are struck by its ring of historical truth.

The Gospels have no surprises for us either in their account of the crucifixion or in their attestation of Jesus' resurrection. After all, the *titulus* above the cross spelled out precisely why Jesus was crucified: He was accused of having proclaimed himself King of the Jews (Matthew 27:37; Mark 15:26; Luke 23:38). *Having been found guilty of treason, was not Jesus fated for crucifixion, the punishment designed especially for those who dared to challenge the authority of Rome?* The *titulus* preserved in the Gospels thus leaves us in no doubt as to *why* Jesus was crucified and *by whom*. And the fact that on either side of him was a revolutionary suffering the same fate evokes for

[3]Josephus invariably uses *lestos* to mean "revolutionary," not "robber."

us Rome's determination to eradicate anyone who challenged its rule, whether violent revolutionary or charismatic visionary.

Jesus' last words as reported in the Gospels (Mark 15:34) likewise come to us as no surprise. These are words that might very well have sprung to the lips of a charismatic when confronted with the implications of his approaching death. Sharing the belief held by all Jews that the Messiah would bring in the kingdom of God during his time on earth, a charismatic would realize, when death was imminent, that his messianic hopes had been dashed. Every would-be messiah knew that there was only one test for his claims: Had he or had he not brought in the kingdom of God in his lifetime? His own demise, whether by the sword or by the cross, would bring an end to his messianic pretensions. When, therefore, a charismatic found himself at death's door, the frightening thought that God had misled him was bound to well up within him. Twisted with pain beyond endurance, his tragic plight would evoke the Psalmist's cry, so expressive of his own feelings of wretched wonder: "My God, my God, why hast thou forsaken me?"

Christians understandably interpret the meaning of this verse differently. For Christians, the Gospels are the repository of the living Christ fused with a Jesus who lived, preached, healed the sick, exorcised demons, sat with sinners, turned the other cheek, clashed with the Pharisees, and underwent a trial, a condemnation, and a crucifixion prior to being seen risen from the dead by his disciples. Few indeed are the Christians who would deny the historical value of the Gospel accounts, even though they may point out that the historical Jesus is beyond our direct knowledge. However Christians might evaluate the historicity of Jesus, all would agree that the historical Jesus is but a limited aspect of Jesus Christ's importance for them. Christianity is not about the man, though man he was as well, but about the Jesus who is the Christ because he rose from the dead. It was only because Jesus was the Christ and not just Jesus, a charismatic of charismatics, that he became the focus of the Gospels. As the risen Christ, Jesus' historical destiny lies in his elevation above history.

The Gospel writers thus tell us of this Jesus Christ who must have been aware that he would rise from the dead even while he was still alive. Indeed, he had made known to his disciples, however veiled the allusions, that he would rise from the dead—allusions that his disciples may not have understood at the time. When, therefore, he cried out from the cross "My God, my God, why hast thou forsaken me?" the Gospel writers, viewing Jesus' life and crucifixion in light of the resurrection that had already occurred for them, could not possibly take Jesus' cry literally. Jesus as the Christ of the Evangelists must surely have known that God had not forsaken him.

The non-Christian historian has no means for weighing and measuring the facts as attested to by faith. When, therefore, he deduces a charismatic of charismatics from the writings of Josephus, he is limited in his deductions—deductions about the way this charismatic of charismatics would have responded to his imminent death—by his knowledge of what was anticipated from a Messiah by the Jews of Jesus' day. The historian cannot know of a messianic belief that requires a death followed by a resurrection to prove one's messianic claims until such a belief emerges for the first time in the history of the messianic idea. Even the disciples of Jesus had to wait three days following his crucifixion before they witnessed the risen Jesus. The historian can, perhaps, anticipate a quantum leap into novelty, but he cannot know what this novelty will actually consist of until the leap has occurred. Lacking this foreknowledge, the historian has no choice other than to read these words of Jesus on the cross as among the most pathetic ever uttered in the annals of history.

We thus face an unbridgeable chasm—a chasm separating the charismatic of charismatics drawn by a non-Christian historian based on the writings of Josephus from the Jesus who proved himself to be the Christ through his resurrection, a resurrection attested to by his disciples but neither attested to nor believed by any known Scribe-Pharisee other than Paul.

This chasm that separates the historical Jesus from Jesus the risen Christ is wide and deep. It cannot be bridged by the historian because he has no criteria by which the testimony of faith can be weighed and measured. It is a chasm that the historian should not cross because he cannot cross it. When, therefore, he points out that within the Synoptic Gospels that were written to record the teachings, the preachings, the wondrous acts, and the life odyssey of Jesus the risen Christ he can also find a Jesus who resembles the portrait of the charismatic of charismatics drawn from Josephus, the historian is thereby neither displacing nor passing judgment on the portraits found in the Gospels. For Christians, the Gospel portraits of the Christ are historically true since they were drawn not simply from life but from Life. As such, they are portraits in which the this-worldly features of Jesus the charismatic are subordinated to the otherworldly features of Jesus the Christ who rose from the dead.

As a non-Christian historian, I have merely attempted to compare the this-worldly features found within the Synoptic Gospels with those features that resemble the portrait of a charismatic of charismatics drawn from Josephus. Such a comparison reveals that though the Gospel writers are drawing portraits of Jesus the risen Christ, they have included within those portraits a picture of a historical Jesus. The Gospels thus turn out to be precious sources for our knowledge both of the historical Jesus and of Jesus the risen Christ.

Even the witnessing of Jesus risen from the dead, with the new meaning of the Messiah to which it gave birth, lay deep though dormant in the womb of Pharisaism. After all, the Scribes-Pharisees daily had taught that every righteous individual would some day be rewarded by being raised from the dead. Resurrection was not only possible but inevitable. This was the very belief the Gospels tell us was preached during his lifetime by Jesus himself—the belief that even gained him much praise from a Scribe who was so pleased with Jesus' artful use of a proof-text from Scripture to confute the Sadducees, who did not believe in resurrection. The historical Jesus had seeded in the minds of his disciples the absolute certainty that resurrection would someday occur. When, therefore, these disciples saw their Master and Teacher dead on the cross, when their faith in his claims were being so violently assaulted by the seeming fact of his death, their eyes were already open to believe what they were to see only three days later: Jesus fully alive as the Christ. Since the fact of resurrection was for them, as for the Scribes-Pharisees, not only possible but inevitable, they did not brush aside what they saw as a fantasy, an illusion, or a wish fulfillment. Rather, they saw in the risen Christ the absolute proof that Jesus must be the Messiah—a proof that was there for all except those blinded by faithlessness to see.

We thus have found within the Gospels a historical Jesus, however subordinated he may be to Jesus the risen Christ. That historical Jesus is the Jesus whose features are identical to those of the charismatic of charismatics drawn from Josephus. In our reconstruction, we do not draw upon those features that are not identical, though we make no claim that there are not other such features as well. Bound only by the portrait of the charismatic of charismatics we have drawn from Josephus, we have freely searched these features out in all the Gospels, irrespective of the time they were written and their differing perspectives.

And that historical Jesus who peers forth in the Gospel stories is the same Jesus who followed John the Baptist; who reached lovingly to the poor and the wretched; who healed the sick, exorcised demons, broke bread with sinners, stood his ground against the Scribes-Pharisees, spoke in parables, preached an ethic and a morality that seemed to defy human nature; who proclaimed that the kingdom of God was at hand and that the time for making oneself ready was short; who intimated that he might indeed be the Son of man, the Messiah whom God had selected to usher in his kingdom and had invested with an authority that freed him from the strictures of the Scribes-Pharisees; who cried out against all those who blocked the way to God's kingdom and turned over the tables of the money changers in the Temple in a fit of religious zeal; who attracted crowds with the eloquence of his teaching and preaching and stirred up the fears of the high priest that these crowds might get out of hand; who was arrested by orders of the high priest and was tried by the high priest's sanhedrin for the political implications of his nonviolent, nonpolitical teaching and preaching; who was brought before Pontius Pilate, the only authority with the power to determine his ultimate fate; who died an agonizing death on the cross, positioned between two revolutionaries, with the words "My God, my God, why hast thou forsaken me?" on his lips; who was seen risen from the dead by his faithful disciples who had heard him speak time and time again of the resurrection that awaited all those who heeded God's Word; and who, once risen, was proclaimed to be the Christ who would soon be bringing the kingdom of God.

This, we can suggest, is the historical Jesus that is to be found in the Gospels, and it is one and the same as the charismatic of charismatics we have deduced from Josephus. Not simply a charismatic but a charismatic of charismatics—one of those rare spirits who burst into this world at infrequent intervals to confront ordinary humans and mere charismatics with a life that is out of this world, and a love that is out of this world, and a hope that is out of this world. And because such a one is out of this world, there are few who can emulate his life or his Life. The world closes in and spreads a veil of human frailties over him, leaving, even in the records of his life, only shadows of that life in this world. For had Jesus not been a spirit so rare when he walked among men, would his life not have ended with death rather than with Life?

WHAT CRUCIFIED JESUS?

Throughout the centuries, Jews and Christians have struggled with the Gospel legacy. As the only record of Jesus' life, ministry, trial, crucifixion, and attested resurrection, it has been cherished by believing Christians just as the story of Moses in the Pentateuch has been cherished by believing Jews. Just as Jesus is reported in the Gospel of Matthew (5:17–18) to have told his followers that he had come not to abolish the Law but to fulfill it, so Christian ministers have preached to their flocks that not one iota, not one dot of the Gospel story will pass away until all that is taught within it is accomplished. So trustworthy indeed was the record for believing Christians that they could offer no more powerful attestation to the veracity of any statement than to affirm it as "gospel" truth.

However, what was gospel truth for Christians was gospel untruth for Jews. Until very recent times, all Jews regarded the Gospels as false revelation and looked upon Jesus as a false messiah. For Jews, the Gospels seemed to be the source of their tragic experience with Christians not only throughout the Middle Ages but into modern times as well. Jews found in the Gospels the source of the harassments, the humiliations, the pogroms, and the expulsions that have plagued them to this day, the day of the Holocaust. Indeed, there are many Jews who are convinced that anti-Semitism will never pass away until every jot and tittle of the Gospel stories is erased. As long as Christians read in the Gospels of Jesus' denunciation of the Scribes-Pharisees as hypocrites, whitewashed tombs, venemous vipers, and sons of hell (Matthew 23:13–33); as long as Christians read as gospel truth the cry "Crucify him" shouted by the Jews before Pilate (Mark 15:13; cf. Matthew 27:22, Luke 23:21, John 19:6) or the insistence of the Jews that Pilate should crucify Jesus because "We have a law, and by that law he ought to die because he has made himself Son of God" (John 19:7), anti-Semitism is the cross that Jews living among Christians will be forced to bear.

Some salvation for Jews seemed to be at hand with the spread of critical biblical scholarship in the nineteenth and twentieth centuries. Non-Jewish scholars, many of them Christians, subjected the Gospel accounts to scrutiny and concluded that however much truth they might contain, the Gospel stories fall far short of being the gospel truth. Although some of those non-Jewish scholars may have been anti-Semitic and most of them looked upon Christianity as a higher stage of religion than Judaism, they nonetheless opened the sluice gates for challenge of the Gospels. Indeed, some went so far as to raise the question of whether a Jesus had actually lived. If the Gospels, then, were not gospel truth, the harsh anti-Jewish passages in the New Testament could be ascribed to the long, tortuous process by which the earliest traditions about Jesus were amplified, expanded, even negated by the changing needs of the Christian communities as they spread into the gentile world. Jesus' hostility toward Jews that emanates from the Gospels could be mitigated by transferring that hostility from Jesus to the Gospel writers, writers who had attributed to the historical Jesus the hostile feelings of a later age.

Yet there are empirical facts that cannot be dissolved. Only if we were to agree with those few scholars who question whether there was a Jesus could we dodge the facts that Jesus was tried, crucified, and seen by his followers as resurrected during the procuratorship of Pontius Pilate and the high priesthood of Caiaphas. And if these bare facts are true, then the question of responsibility is certain to be raised again and again. For Jesus was no ordinary man, and his crucifixion and attested resurrection were no ordinary events. His life, his trial, his crucifixion, and the faith in his resurrection launched a religion of enormous profundity and power. For his followers, his life, trial, crucifixion, and rising from the dead were facts before which all other facts must bow. And of all these facts *for faith*, the fact of his resurrection is the fact nonpareil, for without that belief, however visualized, there would have been no Christianity. Had Jesus' life ended with death, his fate would have been no different from that of John the Baptist—no matter how many withered arms he had healed, how many demons he had exorcised, or how many wretched he had comforted. It was only because his life ended in Life that Christianity was endowed with life. But without the claim that he was the Son of man, the King-Messiah, and without the crucifixion that followed from that claim, there could have been no resurrection. So whatever the findings of critical scholarship, a triad of facts—trial, crucifixion, attested resurrection—undergird Christianity.

The collision between Jews and Christians over the facts that revolve around Jesus as the Messiah and around Jesus' resurrection is a collision that should no longer be necessary. Although the wish to spread the good news about Jesus and the good news about Judaism is not only understandable but desirable, the likelihood that Jews will ever accept the resurrection as a fact or that believing Christians will ever be convinced that the resurrection did not occur is remote indeed. As faith communities, Judaism and Christianity follow paths that do not intersect.

But when it comes to the trial and crucifixion, collision between Jews and Christians would seem to be inevitable. The Gospels have drawn up a bill of indictment, an indictment that is bound to provoke the question Who crucified Jesus? And once the question is thus phrased, we instinctively focus on the persons responsible. And those persons are seen to be, with the exception of Pontius Pilate, Jews. *But should our focus shift from casting blame on persons to casting blame on the time, the place, and the situation, we may be able to view the issue in a new light.* Perhaps it was not *who* one was but *what* one was that is the crux. *For it emerges with great clarity, both from Josephus and from the Gospels. that the culprit is not the Jews but the Roman imperial system.* It was the Roman emperor who appointed the procurator; it was the procurator who appointed the high priest; and it was the high priest who convoked his privy council. It was the Roman imperial system that exacted harsh tribute. It was the actions of Roman procurators that drove the people wild and stirred Judea with convulsive violence. And it was the Roman imperial system that bred revolutionaries and seeded charismatics.

It was the Roman imperial system that was at fault, not the system of Judaism. The Sadducees, Scribes-Pharisees, and Essenes pushed no one to violent revolt, sowed no soil to breed charismatics. Neither biblical writ nor Oral Law allowed for the high priest to be elevated into or tossed out of the high priestly office at the whim of puppet king or arrogant procurator. Nor was there to be found in either the Written or Oral Law any provision for the high priest to convoke a sanhedrin for any purpose whatsoever. So far removed in that day were the Sadducees, Scribes-Pharisees, and Essenes from punitive actions against those who might preach aberrant ideas that the Scribes-Pharisees allowed Sadducean high priests to enter the Holy of Holies on the Day of Atonement, provided they followed Pharisaic procedures. And they allowed Sadducees to preach their heretical views, provided they did not act them out publicly.

And insofar as the *bet din* (*boulé*) of the Pharisees was concerned, it exercised jurisdiction only over those who freely chose to follow the teachings of the Scribes-Pharisees, over the conduct of public worship, and over the liturgical calendar. Not only was the *bet din* a *boulé* and not a sanhedrin, but it was presided over by a nasi, not the high priest, and it consisted exclusively of teachers of the twofold Law. Had there been no Roman imperial system, Jesus would have faced the buffetings of strong words, the batterings of skillfully aimed proof-texts, and the ridicule of both Sadducees and Scribes-

Pharisees, but he would have stood no trial, been affixed to no cross.

And what is striking is that the Gospels confirm that no institution of Judaism had anything to do with the trial and crucifixion of Jesus. We find in the Gospels that the high priest was appointed in violation of both the onefold and the twofold Law; that the high priest's sanhedrin convoked by him had no warrant from either the onefold or the twofold Law; that the procurator was appointed by Rome, with no sanction from either the onefold or the twofold Law; and that the penalty of crucifixion was nowhere provided for in either the onefold or the twofold Law. One searches in the Gospels for the *bet din* (*boulé*) of the Scribes-Pharisees; for the nasi who presided over it; for the procedures spelled out by either the Written or the Oral Law; for the specific Written or Oral Law that Jesus had violated, but all in vain.

What we do find is that Joseph of Arimathea, a member of the *boulé—not* the sanhedrin—seeks to give Jesus a Jewish burial (Mark 15:43; cf. Luke 23:50); that the nasi Gamaliel urges the sanhedrin to let Peter and his associates go free (Acts 5:34 ff.); that Paul disrupts a sanhedrin when the Pharisees support his belief in resurrection (Acts 23:6–10); and that Jesus is seen risen from the dead, as the core teaching of the Scribes-Pharisees allowed.

It is true that the Gospels portray the Scribes-Pharisees as challenging Jesus' claims, and it is true that the Scribes-Pharisees are pictured as cooperating with the authorities, but that is a far cry from having religious jurisdiction. The Scribes-Pharisees confronted the Sadducees with no less angry, harsh, even vituperative words—but words only. And as for the Scribes-Pharisees' cooperation with the authorities, such cooperation was not a result of concern about the religious consequences but about the tragic *political* consequences that could befall the entire Jewish people.

And those political consequences could be devastating indeed. Thousands of Jews had lost their lives only a few years before in the aftermath of the pulling down of the golden eagle. Uncounted others had been slain in bloody encounters between religiously motivated procurators and puppet kings. Rulers in Jesus' day knew that prophetic visions were not to be trifled with, just as they had known it in the days of Jeremiah. Frightened by the crowds drawn to Jesus' charisma and absolutely certain themselves that Jesus was not the messiah and that the kingdom of God was not at hand, some Scribes-Pharisees may have voiced their concern about the tragic consequences that might follow should the crowds get out of hand and go on a rampage. They reasoned, even as Herod the Tetrarch had reasoned, that it was risky to take chances when the stakes were so high. There may have been a sharing of these concerns—concerns that did not arise from the religious content of Jesus' teachings but from their political implications for the authorities. The Scribes-Pharisees, after all, were committed to *both* the doctrine of live and let live in the religious sphere and the doctrine of the two realms in the political sphere.

It is this doctrine of render unto Caesar the things that are Caesar's and unto God the things that are God's that was the gut issue. It was a doctrine that the Scribes-Pharisees, the Sadducees, and the Essenes all subscribed to because it held out the hope of the preservation of the people of Israel as a people of God. The essence of that designation was the covenant that had been made with God, not with the Roman emperor. And that covenant called for obedience to God's revealed Law: the Written Law for the Sadducees; the Written and the Oral Law for the Scribes-Pharisees; the Written Law and other holy writings for the Essenes. As long as that covenant could be kept, the issue of political sovereignty was irrelevant. After all, had not the Aaronide priests, for more than two centuries, tended the altar and preserved the covenant under the imperial sway first of the Persians, then of Alexander, then of the Ptolemies? If the preservation of God's covenant required subservience to Roman rule, the payment of tribute to Rome, or helpless inaction as Roman legions repressed unruly crowds, then this was but a small price to pay for spiritual survival. It was not by might or by power but by the Spirit that the people of God were to be sustained.

Render unto Caesar the things that are Caesar's and unto God the things that are God's became no less a fundamental doctrine in early Christianity. Indeed, it was Jesus himself who enunciated it (Mark 12:17; cf. Matthew 22:21, Luke 20:25). Jesus did not call on his followers to withhold tribute from Rome, nor did he call on them to overthrow Roman rule by force. God, not man, would usher in the kingdom. *Jesus, like the Scribes-Pharisees, adhered to the doctrine of the two realms throughout his entire earthly life*. And his followers likewise adhered. For once it became evident that Jesus' Second Coming was to be delayed, the early Christians pleaded with Rome to extend to them the same religious autonomy it had extended to the Jews. As long as the emperor did not obstruct Christians from believing that their Lord and Master had risen from the dead and as long as he did not prohibit the peaceful spreading of the good news among the Jews and pagans of the empire, Christian leaders were willing to urge their followers to pray for the welfare of the emperor, even as the Jews offered sacrifices and prayers for his well-being. The problem for the early Christians was not their unwillingness to make such a compact but the emperor's unwillingness. When that willingness eventually was forthcoming from Constantine, Christian leaders responded with swiftness and relief.

And the reason? The very same that had motivated the Sadducees, the Scribes-Pharisees, and the Essenes. The Christians were *the* people of Christ. They were the true Israel, a people who, like the people of Israel, were sustained not by might or by power but by the Spirit of God. They were a people sojourning in this vale of tears while longing for the eternal life that awaited them beyond the grave. Even when the church became a worldly power, it never ceased preaching the good news that each Christian would find true salvation in the bosom of Christ, not in the bosom of king or emperor.

Therefore, when the Scribes-Pharisees sought to preserve the people of God by setting aside Caesar's turf for Caesar and God's turf for God, they were pointing the way for the Christians to come. *And just as the Scribes-Pharisees were wary of charismatics and would-be messiahs lest their visions unleash violent consequences, so the Christian leaders proved to be wary when this or that individual announced the Second Coming of Christ*. There was this difference, however: The Scribes-Pharisees could voice their concern, but they had no coercive power for the state in Jesus' day was not a "Jewish" state as the states of the Middle Ages were "Christian" states. Only the procurator or the procurator-appointed high priest and his sanhedrin could judge the potential danger inherent in the teachings of a charismatic, order his arrest, bring him to trial, and render a judgment. And the procurator had the right to make the final decision as to that charismatic's fate. From perceived threat until final judgment, political factors alone weighed in the balance. Whatever link there may have been between the Scribes-Pharisees and the political authorities, it was a link that derived from the doctrine of the two realms, not a link that derived from Jesus' "heretical" teachings.

If, then, we are to assess responsibility, we once again find ourselves laying it at the feet of the Roman imperial system, a system that had made the doctrine of the two realms necessary for the survival of Judaism. The times were no ordinary times; the tempests no ordinary tempests; the bedlam no ordinary bedlam; the derangements no ordinary derangements. The chaos that gave birth to a charismatic like Jesus was the very chaos that rendered clarity of judgment impossible. The Roman emperor held the life or death of the Jewish people in the palm of his hand; the procurator's sword was always at the ready; the high priest's eyes were always penetrating and his ears always keen; the soldiery was always eager for the slaughter. Jewish religious leaders stumbled dazed from day to day, not knowing what they should do or not do, say or not say, urge or not urge. Everyone was entangled within a web of circumstance from which there was no way out. Whatever one did was wrong; whatever one thought was belied; whatever one hoped for was betrayed. Thrashing about in a world gone berserk and in abysmal ignorance of the outcome of any decision or action, one did what, in one's human frailty, one thought was the right thing to do. The emperor sought to govern an empire; the procurator sought to hold anarchy in check; the high priest sought to hold on to his office; the members of the high priest's sanhedrin sought to spare the people the dangerous consequences of a charismatic's innocent visions of the kingdom of God, which they themselves believed was not really at hand; the Scribes-Pharisees sought to lift up the eyes of the people from the sufferings of this world to the peace of life eternal; the followers of Jesus sought to make sense of the confusion and terror that enveloped the last days of the life of their Master and Teacher.

It is in this maelstrom of time, place, and circumstance, in tandem with impulse-ridden, tempest-tossed, and blinded sons of men, that the tragedy of Jesus' crucifixion is to be found. It was not the Jewish people who crucified Jesus and it was not the Roman people: It was the imperial system, a system that victimized the Jews, victimized the Romans, and victimized the Spirit of God.

And Jesus understood. Twisted in agony on the cross—that symbol of imperial Roman cruelty and ruthless disregard of the human spirit—Jesus lifted his head upward toward God and pleaded, "Father, forgive them; for they know not what they do" (Luke 23:34).

II
LOCATING JOHN THE BAPTIST IN PALESTINIAN JUDAISM

The Political Dimension

A paper delivered at the Society of Biblical Literature Meeting (Dallas, TX), December 1983. Published in S.B.L. Seminar Papers, 1983.

In Book XVIII:116–119 of *Antiquities*, Josephus draws a touching vignette of John the Baptist:

> But to some of the Jews the destruction of Herod's army seemed to be divine vengeance, and certainly a just vengeance, for his treatment of John, surnamed the Baptist. For Herod had put him to death, though he was a good man and had exhorted the Jews to live righteous lives, to practice justice toward their fellows and piety toward God, and [in] so doing join in baptism. In his view, this was a necessary preliminary if baptism was to be acceptable to God. They must not employ it to gain pardon for whatever sins they committed but as a consecration of the body, implying that the soul was already thoroughly cleansed by right behavior. When others, too, joined the crowds about him because they were aroused to the highest degree by his sermons [words], Herod became alarmed. Eloquence that had so great an effect on mankind might lead to some form of sedition for it looked as if they would be guided by John in everything they did.
>
> Herod decided, therefore, that it would be much better to strike first and be rid of him before his work led to an uprising than to wait for an upheaval, get involved in a difficult situation, and see his mistake. Though John [was put to death], . . . the verdict of the Jews was that the destruction visited upon Herod's army was a vindication of John, since God saw fit to inflict such a blow on Herod.

Josephus pictures John the Baptist as a nonpolitical religious reformer. He is stirred by the sinfulness of the people to exhort them to lead virtuous lives and to practice justice toward their fellows and piety toward God. To this end he calls upon them to cleanse their souls with righteousness and consecrate the body with baptism. He was a good man, interested in arousing the people to repentance and not to violence. If any political transformations followed, these transformations would reveal the hand of God and not the hand of man.

Yet John the Baptist so frightened Herod Antipas the Tetrarch (4 B.C.E.–39 C.E.) that he had John put to death. And the reason? His teachings were so eloquent that they attracted crowds—and crowds were dangerous, even if John was not stirring them up to revolt against Roman authority. Herod could take no chances lest a failure to act decisively on his part lead to a violent demonstration and his own undoing.

Herod's harsh and brutal decision shocked the people at large. John the Baptist was no violent revolutionary. He was no rabble-rouser. He was a voice crying in the wilderness: "Repent of your sins, cleanse yourselves with virtue and righteousness." So high indeed was John held in the eyes of the people that they explained the defeat of Herod's army as a vindication of John's goodness, virtue, and righteousness. And to this explanation Josephus gives his assent.

Josephus's vignette of John the Baptist is brief but it is revealing. It is revealing in that it shows that Josephus, with all of his presumed pro-Roman bias, was sympathetic to John. He shared with the people at large their shock that so virtuous, righteous, and pious a charismatic as John should have been treated as though he were some violent revolutionary. And it is also revealing because it compels us to look to that larger framework of fear, violence, and desperation that sealed the fate first of John the Baptist and then of Jesus of Nazareth.

This maelstrom of fear, violence, and desperation that was to seed Judea with the grapes of wrath was already brewing in the last years of Herod's reign, even though it was not brought to completion until the Roman emperors discarded royal pawns for imperial procurators. While Herod the Great (37–4 B.C.E.) lay dying, several young firebrands, stirred by the fulminations of two sages, Judas, the son of Caiphaeus, and Matthias, the son of Margalus, climbed the Temple gate and hacked down the golden eagle that Herod had erected as a symbol of loyalty to Rome. Enraged, Herod had the sages along with their disciples burnt alive (*The Jewish War* I: 648–655; *Antiquities*, XVII:149–167).

The anger felt toward Herod for the burning of these martyrs remained suppressed as long as Herod remained alive, but it burst out in frightening violence only a few days after he drew his last breath. Seeking to win the affection and loyalty of the people, Herod's son, Archelaus, addressed them and promised to heed the petitions that they had submitted to him. Nevertheless, a large assembly of Jews gathered in the Temple area and began a lamentation bewailing the fate of those whom Herod had punished for cutting down the golden eagle at the gate of the Temple.

"This mourning," Josephus tells us, "was in no subdued tones: There were piercing shrieks, a dirge directed by a conductor, and lamentations with beating of the breast, which resounded throughout the city; all this in honor of the unfortunate men who, they asserted, had in defense of their country's laws and the Temple perished on the pyre. These martyrs ought, they clamored, to be avenged by the punishment of Herod's favorites, and the first step was the deposition of the high priest whom he had appointed, as they had a right to select a man of greater piety and purer morals" (*The Jewish War* II: 6–9).

So wrought up were the mourners that Archelaus's efforts to calm them down met with violent resistance. And when Archelaus became frightened that the multitudes that were then gathering for Passover might follow the lead of the dissidents, he sent a tribune in command of a cohort to restrain them by force. The crowds responded violently, pelting the cohort with stones and killing most of them. Archelaus, recognizing that bloodshed could not be avoided, let loose his entire army, including cavalry, upon the various parties busy with their sacrifices and slew about three thousand of them (Ibid., 8:15; cf. *Antiquities* XVII: 206 ff.).

The incident of the golden eagle ushered in a reign of violence, death, destruction, and despair that was not overthrown until the Romans had butchered countless numbers of Jews, laid waste to Jerusalem, burned the Temple, and carted off thousands to be sold into slavery. "What was there, then, about this incident," we must ask, "that could trigger such a reign of violence?"

On the face of it, we find two interlocked components: a religious component and a political component. The sages, who were agitated over the golden eagle, saw in the eagle an idolatrous image. By contrast, Herod, and those who sided with him, looked upon the golden eagle as an innocuous symbol of political loyalty and not an object of religious worship at all. For Herod, the golden eagle was not the same as the images or busts of the emperors. In his eyes the golden eagle was no different from the cherubim that God himself had commanded to be put in the Tabernacle. The eagle was nothing but a symbol of the compact that regulated the relationship between Rome and the Jewish people: In return for Rome's exempting the Jews from the obligation to erect statues of the emperors in the Temple, the Jews acknowledged the legitimacy of Roman rule. Herod, therefore, looked upon the cutting down of the eagle as a political act of defiance masking as religious piety. And this opinion seems to have been shared by the Jewish leaders who sided with Herod on this issue. For them, too, the eagle was simply a sign of the covenant with Rome as summed up in the formula "Render unto Caesar what is Caesar's and unto God what is God's."

Nonetheless, it is evident from the violent demonstrations that occurred after Herod's death that a large number of Jews did regard the erection of the golden eagle as a violation of that compact. For them the eagle was in fact equivalent to the icons of the emperors that the emperors had agreed not to set up in the Temple or parade through the city of Jerusalem.

Clearly this was a murky issue, one that could be viewed either as religious *or* political, depending on one's interpretation. And it was this murkiness that plunged Judea into a maelstrom of violence and prompted Herod the Tetrarch to put John the Baptist to death and Pontius Pilate to condemn Jesus of Nazareth to the cross.

The violence unleashed by the incident of the golden eagle let loose a spate of dissidence and violence all the while that the emperor Augustus was pondering how best to govern Herod's kingdom now that Herod was dead. Especially frightening was the tenacity that the Jews displayed when they rose up against Sabinus, a Roman official who had provoked the people by seeking to gain access to the royal treasures during the festival of Passover in 4 B.C.E. So successfully indeed did they hold Sabinus and his soldiers under siege that it was not until Varus, the procurator of Syria, came with reinforcements that the Jews finally gave in. In the meantime the Roman legionaries had set fire to the magnificent porticoes, adding fuel to the enflamed feelings of the Jews toward their Roman rulers (*Antiquities* XVIII: 250–298).

Although less dramatic, the other disturbances that required Varus's forceful intervention reveal how tempest-tossed the people were. At Sepphoris in Galilee, Judas, the son of Ezekias, a vintage revolutionary, raised a band of followers who broke open the royal arsenals to arm themselves against rival groupings (*Antiquities* XVII: 271–272); in Peraea, a certain Simon made a bid for royal power by burning down the royal palace at Jericho along with other stately mansions; and elsewhere, Anthrongaeus, a shepherd, seeded his own furrows of violence in an effort to gain the crown for himself. Although ultimately put down, these usurpers had set a patten for guerrilla warfare that was to become endemic (Ibid., 273–277).

Faced with an unruly people and concerned over the high cost of keeping the peace, the emperor Augustus decided to break up Herod's kingdom and assign Judea to a Roman administrator. In doing so, he unwittingly ushered in an era of permanent revolution. Hitherto the peace had been more or less assured by the three "philosophies" or "schools of thought" of Judaism that had come to adhere to the doctrine of two realms: a political realm and a religious realm. So long as the political authorities did not intrude into the realm of God, the religious leaders would not intrude into the realm of Caesar. This compact hearkened back to the latter years of the Hasmoneans, when it became evident to the Sadducees and Pharisees alike that the politicizing of religion could only lead to the kind of terror and counterterror that had marked the reign and high priesthood of Alexander Janneus, who had identified his cause with the Sadducees, and the reign of Salome Alexandra, who had identified her cause with the Pharisees. Although Pharisees and

Sadducees may have continued to be involved with politics, such an involvement did not carry with it the suppression of the Sadducees by the Pharisees or the Pharisees by the Sadducees, even though in matters of public worship and in matters affecting the liturgical calendar the Pharisaic dispensation was followed. A spirit of live and let live permeated the day-to-day relationship between the "philosophies," as is evident from the fact that the Pharisees were willing to countenance high priests who were Sadducees and from the fact that the Sadducees were willing to follow Pharisaic procedures when carrying out their duties in the Temple.

The clearest sign that the Sadducees and Pharisees had committed themselves to the doctrine of the two realms was the fact that they raised no clamor when Herod decided to appoint the high priest and to keep the high priest's vestments under lock and key. Although there could be no religious justification for a high priest appointed by the ruler, they did not disqualify him so long as his public performance did not violate the procedures as set forth by the Pharisees. As far as the Sadducees and the Pharisees were concerned, the high priest had become a political figure whose religious functions in the Temple were pro forma and nominal. The religious legitimacy of the high priest was, it seemed, a small price to pay for the promise on the part of the political authorities to allow the "philosophies" to have full autonomy in the religious sphere.

This compact with the state was endangered, however, when the first procurator decreed that a census be taken to determine the amount of tribute the Jews would have to pay. Although the leaders of the Sadducees and the Pharisees, mindful of the compact, urged the people to knuckle under, a certain Judas of Galilee and Zadok the Pharisee refused on the grounds that "the assessment carried with it a status amounting to downright slavery and on the grounds that Heaven would be their zealous helper." So principled was their stand that although they agreed with the "philosophy" of the Pharisees in all other respects, they broke off from them because they, unlike the Pharisees, refused to call anyone but God Ruler, *Hegemon*, or *Despotes* (Emperor). Thus was born what Josephus called a Fourth Philosophy. And with the birth of this Fourth Philosophy, the era of permanent revolution was ushered in (*Antiquities* XVIII: 1–25).

The rise of the Fourth Philosophy thus shattered what had been until then a mosaic of Judaism. Sadducees, Pharisees, Essenes, despite the unbridgeable chasm that separated them on fundamental doctrinal issues, had come to accept the doctrine of the two realms and the doctrine of live and let live. Not so the Fourth Philosophy. Their leaders insisted that political sovereignty could not be sealed off from divine sovereignty. For them, the payment of tribute was to recognize the Roman emperor as a god and not simply as a king of flesh and blood. There could be no line separating the religious from the political. To overthrow Rome was a divine imperative no less demanding of fulfillment than any other command of God.

With the rise of the Fourth Philosophy, the Romans could no longer look upon the "philosophies" of Judaism as a mosaic of loyalty but as a seedbed of revolution. The markers sharply setting off the turf of Caesar from the turf of God had been uprooted. All religious teachings were now suspect. All religious teachers were now under scrutiny. Revolution and sedition could not be allowed to be masked as righteousness and piety.

The Roman authorities and the high priests whom they appointed to be their eyes and ears were thus ready to deal as harshly with the nonviolent dissidents who were cropping up as with the followers of the Fourth Philosophy. Prophets and charismatics in their own way could prove to be even more dangerous than the violent ones.

Visions of God's power sweeping away the princes, kings, and emperors of this world to make way for the glorious end of days when God's Anointed would rule were not the stock-in-trade of revolutionaries like Judas and Zadok but of prophetlike dreamers and charismatics who were simple believers in the power of repentance, of virtue, of righteousness, and of purity of soul to arouse God to do wonders for his people and bring to an inglorious end the harsh sovereignties of this world.

Josephus tells us of the fear that the prophets, visionaries, and charismatics aroused:

> Besides these [the so-called Sicarii who committed murders in broad daylight in the heart of the city and who were responsible for the assassination of the high priest Jonathan] there arose another body of villains, with purer hands but more impious intentions, who no less than the assassins ruined the peace of the city.

> Deceivers and imposters, under the pretence of divine inspiration fostering revolutionary changes, they persuaded the multitude to act like madmen and led them out into the desert under the belief that God would give them tokens of deliverance (*The Jewish War* II:258–260).

As an example of such "prophetic" troublemakers, Josephus tells of an Egyptian "who had gained for himself the reputation of a prophet" and who succeeded in arousing twenty thousand Jews, leading them by a circuitous route from the desert to the Mount of Olives, from which point he planned to force entry into Jerusalem. Before he could implement his plan, however, the troops of the procurator attacked and made short shrift of this "prophetic" challenge (Ibid., 261–265).

Theudas, according to Josephus, was another troublemaker. He claimed that he was a prophet and that at his command the Jordan would be parted. He convinced a large number of Jews to follow him, only to have his claim shattered by a squadron of cavalry that slew many of his followers and took him off to Jerusalem, where he was beheaded (*Antiquities* XX: 97–99).

The decision of Augustus to bring Judea directly under Roman rule thus cracked the mosaic of Judaism and erased the marker separating the realm of Caesar from the realm of God. The Fourth Philosophy preached revolutionary violence in the name of the Lord. Prophets and charismatics likewise preached the coming of God's kingdom in the name of the Lord. It was evident that irrespective of *how* the rule of Rome was to be terminated, a larger and larger number of Jews were willing to listen to leaders offering alternatives to the traditional doctrine of the two realms. Crowds quickly gathered around anyone offering some way out of their anguish, despair, and helplessness, and crowds by their nature were volatile and unpredictable. Once the boundaries between the political and the religious boundaries had been removed, even the most innocent call for repentance, for piety, for righteousness, for justice, for sanctification could be heard by those in authority as a call for the overthrow of Rome. Every religious teacher who deviated the slightest from the doctrine of the two realms as articulated by the Sadducees, Pharisees, and Essenes was a potential revolutionary, since the prophetic call to repentance, to righteousness, to justice, and to sanctification by the great prophets of old—Isaiah, Jeremiah, Ezekiel—had carried with it the promise of the restoration of God's sovereignty over his people.

When, therefore, John the Baptist echoed the prophets by calling on the people to repent and live lives of righteousness, justice, and piety, he was, by implication, holding out the hope that if the repentance was sincere and if enough of the people abandoned their sinful ways, God would usher in the glorious end of days envisioned by the grand prophets who had spoken in his name. Herod the Tetrarch thus had good reason to fear the *political* implications of John's religious teachings once it became evident that he was attracting crowds who might in a surge of religious exaltation and zeal act out on the political implications of John's call for repentance and let loose a torrent of revolutionary violence. As Josephus put it, "Herod decided, therefore, that it would be much better to strike first and be rid of him before his work led to an uprising than to wait for an upheaval, get involved in a difficult situation, and see his mistake" (*Antiquities* XVIII: 118). Herod clearly was not interested in *what* John was preaching but only in *how many people* were listening. The issue was not God, repentance, piety, righteousness, sanctification but crowds. Crowds were dangerous even if not a political word was being uttered. Religious teachings became political teachings ipso facto the moment that a scattering of individuals had clustered into a crowd.

The tragic fate of John the Baptist thus foreshadowed the tragic fate of Jesus of Nazareth. Indeed, the web of ultimate tragedy is woven in the warp and woof of the first verses of the Gospel of Mark:

> The beginning of the gospel of Jesus Christ, the Son of God. As it is written in Isaiah the prophet:
>
> " Behold, I send my messenger before thy
> face, who shall prepare thy way;
> the voice of one crying in the wilderness:
> Prepare the ways of the Lord,
> make his paths straight."

> John the baptizer appeared in the wilderness, preaching a baptism of repentance for the forgiveness of sins. And they went out to him all the country of Judea and all the people of Jerusalem; and they were baptized by him in the river Jordan, confessing their sins.
>
> Now John was clothed with camel's hair and had a leather girdle around his waist and ate locusts and wild honey. And he preached, saying, "After me comes he who is mightier than I, the thong of whose sandals I am not worthy to stoop down and untie. I have baptized you with water; but he will baptize you with the Holy Spirit. . ."
>
> Now after John was arrested, Jesus came into Galilee preaching the gospel of God and saying, "The time is fulfilled, and the kingdom of God is at hand; repent and believe in the gospel" (Mark: 1–8, 14).

John's preaching a baptism of repentance and forgiveness of sins proved to be lethal. Crowds had gathered round him, and crowds were dangerous. The fact that John was calling for repentance from sins and not for revolt against Rome, for forgiveness of sins and not for the head of the emperor was irrelevant to those charged with political responsibility. The only fact that was relevant was whether the voice was a voice crying in the wilderness with no one listening or whether it was a voice crying in a wilderness full of people whose teeth were on edge, whose nerves were frayed, and whose spirits were steeped in despair.

So, too, with Jesus. The moment he preached that the time is fulfilled, that the kingdom of God is at hand, that the people should repent and believe in the gospel, all those charged with political responsibility for Galilee and Judea were looking far more than listening. They were looking to see whether Jesus' preaching was attracting crowds; they were not listening to what he had to say. As soon as it became obvious that large numbers of Jews crowded around Jesus to hear what he had to say, his fate, like John's, was sealed. Crowds, and not the words that aroused them, were all that mattered. Jesus, like John, was put to death not because he was a political agitator or because he challenged the dictum "Render unto Caesar what is Caesar's and unto God what is God's" but because there were no markers any longer separating the turf of Caesar from the turf of God. Even a simple call for repentance was fraught with political danger if too many Jews heeded it.

The tragic fate of John the Baptist thus lays bare the larger tragedy of the Jewish people held tightly in the grip of Rome. From the moment Herod died until the last defendant of Masada had breathed his last, there was virtually no day without its demonstration, no week without its disturbance, no month without its riots, and no year without its rebellion. The tribute was harsh, the procurators cruel and provocative, and the remedies—nostrums all. Driven to the edge of despair and beyond, Jews in ever larger numbers splintered off from the mosaic of Judaism that had kept the peace in Herod's day and kicked the traces, either by following the revolutionary path of the Fourth Philosophy or by putting their faith in prophets and charismatics who promised that God's kingdom was near at hand if only the people repented and purified their lives from sin.

Confronted by dissidence, disorder, and violence, the Roman authorities were at a loss as to what to do. The Jews had proved to be ungovernable. Chaos and anarchy, not the Roman imperium, ruled over Judea and Galilee. As a consequence, everyone charged with political authority was on razor's edge. To make distinctions between a nonpolitical charismatic like John the Baptist or Jesus on the one hand and Judas of Galilee on the other or to discriminate between the shadings of difference between a John the Baptist or a Jesus on the one hand and a Theudas on the other was simply too risky and dangerous. "When in doubt, execute" was seemingly the only secure policy to follow.

This was the reasoning that lay behind Herod the Tetrarch's decision to put "harmless" John to death. This also was the reasoning behind the decision of Caiaphas and Pontius Pilate to put "harmless" Jesus to death. Prophetic revivalism was fraught with political risk. So long as the Romans demanded that the tribute be paid "come hell or high water," hell and high water did indeed come upon the Romans and upon the Jews, and upon John the Baptist and Jesus of Nazareth.

III

AS TO THE LAW A PHARISEE

Paul's Roots in Rabbinic Judaism

A paper delivered at the Society of Biblical Literature, November 1978.

Paul has left us two tantalizing mementos of his sojourn in Judaism. One of these is recorded in Galatians 1:

> For I would have you know, brethren [he admonishes the Galatians who are being seduced by the preachers of a false gospel], "that the gospel that was preached by me is not man's gospel. For I did not receive it from man, nor was I taught it, but it came through a revelation of Jesus Christ. For you have heard of my former life in Judaism, how I persecuted the church of God violently and tried to destroy it; and I advanced in Judaism beyond many of my own age among my people, so extremely zealous was I for the traditions of my Fathers. But when he who had set me apart before I was born and had called me through his grace was pleased to reveal his Son to me in order that I might preach him among the Gentiles, I did not confer with flesh and blood, nor did I go up to Jerusalem to those who were apostles before me, but I went away into Arabia; and again I returned to Damascus (Galatians 1:11–17).

The other memento is to be found in Paul's letter to the Philippians:

> Look out for the dogs, look out for the evil workers, look out for those who mutilate the flesh. For we are the true circumcision, who worship God in spirit and glory in Christ Jesus and put no confidence in the flesh—though I myself have reason for confidence in the flesh also. If any other man thinks he has reason for confidence in the flesh, I have more: circumcized on the eighth day, of the people of Israel, of the tribe of Benjamin, a Hebrew

> born of the Hebrews; as to the Law a Pharisee, as to zeal a persecutor of the church, as to righteousness under the Law blameless (Philippians 3:2–6).

In these two autobiographical recollections, Paul has revealed all that he needed to reveal to impress upon the Galatians and the Philippians that there was no one who could challenge his rootedness in Judaism or who could match him in his knowledge of the Law. To the Galatians, he writes of his precociousness in the traditions of the Fathers; to the Philippians, he ticks off, one by one, his credentials: "circumcized on the eighth day, of the people of Israel, of the tribe of Benjamin, a Hebrew born of the Hebrews; as to the Law a Pharisee, as to zeal a persecutor of the church, as to righteousness under the Law blameless."

There is nothing casual about these revelations. They are set down with passion and in anger. They are hard-hitting reminders that Paul is no ordinary apostle, no ignorant upstart, no frivolous mocker of the Law and its demands. Indeed, in each recollection, he underscores his zealous persecution of the church as being, like his attachment to the Law, precocious: "I persecuted the church of God violently and tried to destroy it."

Brief though he may be, Paul packs into these few sentences a lifetime of passion, zeal, and determination. Paul's Galatian and Philippian brethren presumably needed no exegesis. Paul's early life in Judaism was presumably known to them. Paul could count upon their knowing what he meant when he referred to the "traditions of my Fathers," and the Philippians understood what he was communicating when he said that he had been "as to the Law a Pharisee" and "as to righteousness under the Law blameless." What the Galatians and the Philippians knew so well we know so poorly. We fumble feebly to find the embedded meaning in what Paul took so completely for granted.

Nor is our task lightened by Paul's use of the expression "as to the Law a Pharisee," for our sources—Josephus, the New Testament, and the tannaitic literature—do not yield a simple and easy definition. The tannaitic sources are especially confusing for they leave us in doubt as to when the Hebrew term *perushim* means "Pharisees" and when the term means "separatists." Scholars, unable to differentiate with certainty as to when *perushim* is to be read with a capital *P* and when it is to be read with a small *p* have, for the most part, rendered *perushim* in Mishnah Hagigah 2:7 as Pharisees. Thus they define the Pharisees as a sect of pietists who are meticulously concerned with the laws of ritual purity and who separate themselves from the less meticulous masses, the *am ha'aretz*. Hence, the Mishnah tells us that the garments of an *am ha'aretz* are a source of *midras*, uncleanness, for Perushim, Pharisees. With such a picture in our minds, Paul's words "as to the Law a Pharisee" conjure up a pietist who strictly observed the laws of ritual purity and who kept his ritual distance from the masses, even as his words "righteousness under the Law blameless" fortify this image by seeming to stress that Paul was the most meticulous Pharisee of them all. They do not evoke an image of Paul striving to earn eternal life for his soul and resurrection for his body. They do not picture for us one who strains to be blameless lest the Heavenly Father condemn his soul to endless torment. They do not image Paul as ripe and ready for the loving, saving, and redeeming Christ.

Yet such an image of Paul would be conjured up if our picture of the Pharisees were drawn exclusively from those tannaitic texts in which the term *perushim* must be Pharisees because they are juxtaposed to Zedukkim, Sadducees. And when this testimony is conjoined with that drawn from Josephus and the New Testament, we are compelled to draw a picture of the Pharisees that has no resemblance to the Perushim in the Hagigah text, cited above. We find not a sect distinguished by its meticulous concern with ritual purity but the authoritative teachers of the twofold Law, the Written and the Oral—authorities who preached the good news that God so loved the individual that he revealed his twofold Law to Israel so that each law-abiding Israelite might gain eternal life for his soul and, at some distant and unknown date, resurrection for his body. If these were the Pharisees, then Paul is telling us that in his former life in Judaism he was straining to attain eternal life and resurrection by living a blameless life under the twofold Law. To be a Pharisee was to strive, day and night, for one's salvation in the world to come. The twofold Law was the way, not the destination.

But before following where such a premise would lead, let me first set down proof-texts from Josephus, the New Testament, and the tannaitic literature that reveal (1) that Pharisees were indeed the authoritative teachers of the twofold Law and (2) that they taught the good news of eternal life and resurrection.

Josephus's most explicit definition of the Pharisees is to be found in *Antiquities* XIII: 297:

> For the present, I wish merely to explain that the Pharisees had transmitted to the people certain laws from the Fathers that are not written down in the Laws of Moses, for which reason they are rejected by the Sadducean group, who hold that only those laws that were written down are to be expounded and those that had been transmitted from the Fathers are not to be observed.

The Pharisees are thus the authoritative teachers of the laws that have been transmitted from the Fathers—laws that have not been written down. They are the expounders of the *paradosis* of the Fathers, the very *paradosis* that Paul so precociously obeyed prior to his transfiguration.

Josephus's testimony to the Pharisaic belief in eternal life and resurrection is found not only in his description of Pharisaic beliefs (*War* II:163, *Ant.* XVIII:12–17) but in his remonstrance on suicide in *War* ("Know you not that they who depart this life in accordance with the law of nature and repay the loan that they received from God, when he who lent it is pleased to reclaim it, win eternal renown; that their houses and families are secure; that their souls, remaining spotless and obedient, are allotted the most holy place in heaven, whence, in the revolution of the ages, they return to find in chaste bodies a new habitation? But as for those who have laid mad hands upon themselves, the darker regions of the nether world receive their souls, and God, their Father, visits upon their posterity the outrageous acts of the parents . . ." [*War* III:374–5]); in his explanation of the rewards awaiting the law-abiding Jew in *Against Apion* ("For those . . . who live in accordance with our laws the prize is not silver or gold, no crown of wild olive or of parsley with any such public mark of distinction. No; each individual, relying on the witness of his own conscience and the lawgiver's prophecy, confirmed by the sure testimony of God, is firmly persuaded that to those who observe the laws and if they must need die for them willingly meet death, God has granted a renewed existence and in the revolution of the ages the gift of a better life . . ." [*Against Apion* II:217b–218]); and in his formulation of Abraham's speech to Isaac as he prepared to offer him up as a sacrifice ("Aye, since thou wast born [out of the course of nature, so] quit thou now this life not by the common road but sped by thine own father on thy way to God, the Father of all, through the rites of sacrifice. He, I ween, accounts it not meet for thee to depart this life by sickness or war or by any of the calamities that commonly befall mankind but amid prayers and sacrificial ceremonies would receive thy soul and keep it near to himself . . ." [*Antiquities* I:228–31]).

Like Josephus, the Gospels reveal that the Pharisees were the authoritative teachers of the twofold Law, the Written Law and the *paradosis* (the Oral Law) of the Elders, and the preachers of the good news of eternal life and resurrection. Thus in Mark 7:5 the Pharisees and the Scribes ask Jesus, "Why do your disciples not live according to the Traditions of the Elders but eat with hands defiled?" To which Jesus responds, after citing Isaiah, "You leave the commandment of God and hold fast the tradition of men" (Mark 7:8). "You have a fine way of rejecting the commandment of God in order to keep your tradition" (7:13).

The Pharisees, so the gloss in Mark 7:3 reassures us, do not eat unless they wash their hands, "observing as they do the Traditions of the Elders."

Matthew (15:2–3,6) likewise reaffirms Mark's linkage of the Pharisees to the *paradosis* of the Elders and has them sitting as of uncontested right in Moses' seat (Matthew 23).

Paul's "as to the Law a Pharisee" and Paul's zealousness for the *paradosis* of the Fathers are thus two ways of saying the same thing: "I was nurtured on the twofold Law as taught by the Pharisees and not on the onefold Law as taught by the Sadducees. And I was so precocious in my adherence to this twofold Law that I could believe that I was beyond reproach. I therefore had every reason to believe that eternal life awaited my soul and resurrection awaited my body as the ultimate reward for my impeccable loyalty."

These teachers of the *paradosis* also teach the belief in the resurrection. Thus Mark (12:28) tells us that a Scribe applauded Jesus' refutation of the Sadducees "who say there is no resurrection" (12:18), while Matthew has the Pharisees impressed by Jesus' putting down of the Sadducees (22:34). Similarly, we read in Acts (23:6–9) how Paul provoked a tussle between the Sadducees and the Pharisees when he blurted out at his trial, "Brethren, I am a Pharisee, a son of Pharisees; with respect to the hope and the resurrection of the dead I am on trial" (Acts 23:6). Following which the author of Acts explains that "the Sadducees say there is no resurrection, nor angel, nor spirit; but the Pharisees acknowledge them all" (23:8).

And when we turn to the tannaitic literature, we discover that here, too, the Pharisees are the teachers of the twofold Law and the preachers of eternal life for the righteous soul and resurrection for its body. That the Pharisees were teachers of the twofold Law is evident from the very few tannaitic texts that juxtapose the Perushim, Pharisees, with the Zedukkim, Sadducees. In one of these controversies the Sadducees berate the Pharisees for asserting that "Holy Scriptures renders the hands unclean." As any student of the Pentateuch is aware, there is no such explicit law in the Pentateuch, nor is there any implicit law that could lead by necessary inference to the conclusion that Holy Scriptures, itself a non-Pentateuchal, nonbiblical term, renders the hands unclean. The Sadducees are thus on secure Pentateuchal ground when they deride the Pharisees for this seemingly bizarre dictum. The Pharisees, for their part, have no qualms since this dictum falls within the category of "the words of the Soferim," which need not be logically deducible from the words of the Pentateuch.

The Pharisees are thus revealed to us as none other than the Soferim, whose teachings enjoy a coequal authority with the Pentateuch and whose authority is self-affirming, self-sustaining, and free of scriptural warrant. These Pharisees-Soferim, in turn, are the bearers of the good news of eternal life for the soul and resurrection for the body, as is evident from the following tannaitic texts. The first is from Mishnah Berachot 9:5:

> All those who used to conclude blessings in the Temple used to say "From everlasting [*minha'olam*] to everlasting." But when the heretics perverted the truth and said there is one world only, they [the scholars] ordained that they should say "from everlasting to everlasting" [*minha'olam ve'ad ha'olam*]; i.e., from this world to the world to come.

The second text is from Mishnah Peah 1:1:

> These are things that a person eats the fruits thereof in this world while the principle remains enduring for him in the world to come.

The third is from Mishnah Sanhedrin 6:2:

> When the [condemned] was about ten cubits away from the stoning chamber, they would say unto him "Confess," since it was the custom of those condemned to death to confess; for whoever confesses has a share in the world to come. For we have found that in the case of Achan, Joshua said to him, "My son, give glory unto the Lord, God of Israel, and give praise unto him [*veten lo todah*]." And Achan answered Joshua and said, "Of a truth, I have sinned against the Lord and this is what I did" (Joshua 7:20).
>
> And how do we know that his confession expiated his sin? For it is said (Joshua 7:25), "And Joshua said, 'Why did you bring trouble on us? The Lord brings trouble on you this day.' " [The meaning is], This day you are troubled, but you are not to be troubled in the world to come.
>
> If the convicted one does not know how to confess, they say to him, "Say [the following]: 'May my death be an expiation for all my transgressions.' "

And the fourth is the well-known dictum:

> All Israel has a share in the world to come except, among others, those who deny that the resurrection of the dead is deducible from the Pentateuch (cf. Mark 12:18–27).
>
> And most tellingly, the belief in the resurrection was thrice daily, four times on the Sabbath, and five times on Yom Kippur, to be affirmed and reaffirmed in the core blessings of the prayer par excellence, the *Amidah* or *Shemoneh Esreh*.

When, therefore, Paul proudly enumerated his credentials to the Philippians and capped them with his assurance that as to the

Law he was a Pharisee and as to righteousness under the Law blameless and when he reminded the Galatians that he had advanced in Judaism beyond many of his own age, so extremely zealous had he been for the *paradosis*, he was conjuring up not Judaism in general, nor Sadduceeism, nor Essenism but one specific form of Judaism to the exclusion of all others, namely, Pharisaism. He was telling the Philippians and the Galatians that he had been a precocious follower of the twofold Law, the Written *and* the Oral; that he had fulfilled the demands of this twofold Law so zealously that he could proclaim himself blameless; and that, by implication, if anyone could have anticipated eternal life for his soul and resurrection for his body, it was he. Paul, in a word, was reminding the Philippians and the Galatians that as a follower of the Pharisees, he was straining for otherworldly salvation. For Paul, this world was but the antechamber to the world to come; the twofold Law laid out the glory road to salvation; and Paul has been, law by law, trodding his way to that blessed world of eternal life.

But Paul's journey was abruptly halted when, on the road to Damascus, he saw the risen Christ. Here was the crucified Jesus, fully alive and reaching to embrace Paul with his undemanding love—the very Jesus who had challenged the authority of the Pharisees and had defied them. Yet here was Jesus resurrected from the dead, seemingly rewarded for his defiance rather than condemned. And if Jesus had indeed risen from the dead, then the Pharisees must be wrong. The twofold Law does not map out the road to eternal life and resurrection, for if it did, then how could Jesus, who had defied these teachers, rise from the dead? But Paul had seen Jesus fully alive and reaching out to him. Christ and not the twofold Law reveals the road, lights up the way, and is the destination. The twofold Law is an obstruction, a snare, and a delusion. It is even an agent provocateur of sin; its promise of salvation fraudulent.

Here, then, is the source of Paul's remarkable critique of the Law in Romans 7:4–25:

> Likewise, my brethren, you have died to the Law through the body of Christ so that you may belong to another, to him who has been raised from the dead in order that we may bear fruit for God. While we were living in the flesh, our sinful passions,

aroused by the Law, were at work in our members to bear fruit for death. But now we are discharged from the Law, dead to that which held us captive, so that we serve not under the old written code but in the new life of the Spirit.

What then shall we say? That the Law is sin? By no means! Yet if it had not been for the Law, I should not have known what it is to covet if the Law had not said, "You shall not covet." But sin, finding opportunity in the commandment, wrought in me all kinds of covetousness. Apart from the Law, sin lies dead. I was once alive apart from the Law, but when the commandment came, sin revived and I died; the very commandment that promised life proved to be death to me. For sin, finding opportunity in the commandment, deceived me and by it killed me. So the Law is holy, and the commandment is holy and just and good.

Did that which is good, then, bring death to me? By no means! It was sin, working death in me through what is good, in order that sin might be shown to be sin and through the commandment might become sinful beyond measure. We know that the Law is spiritual; but I am carnal, sold under sin. I do not understand my own actions. For I do not do what I want, but I do the very thing I hate.

Now if I do what I do not want, I agree that the Law is good. So then it is no longer I that do it but sin that dwells within me. For I know that nothing good dwells within me, that is, in my flesh. I can will what is right, but I cannot do it. For I do not do the good I want, but the evil I do not want is what I do. Now if I do what I do not want, it is no longer I that do it but sin that dwells within me.

So I find it to be a law that when I want to do right, evil lies close at hand. For I delight in the Law of God in my inmost self, but I see in my members another law at war with the law of my mind, making me captive to the law of sin that dwells in my members. Wretched man that I am! Who will deliver me from this body of death? Thanks be to God through Jesus Christ our Lord! So then, I of myself serve the Law of God with my mind, but with my flesh I serve the law of sin.

Here, in Romans 7, we find a gospel unique to Paul. It is nowhere to be found in the Synoptics or in John. The Law, to be sure, might not be binding, but it could not be an agent provocateur of sin. Jesus, to be sure, had risen from the dead to elevate man, who was unaided by divine grace and thus helpless in the face of his primordial impulses. Jesus, to be sure, was the Christ, but his teachings were to be drawn from his life *and* resurrection and not, as with Paul, exclusively from his resurrection.

Paul, who had never known Jesus in his lifetime and who was not one of Jesus' disciples, preached the gospel of mutation. His gospel, and his gospel only, is the quantum jump out of Pharisaic Judaism; for it is his gospel, and his gospel alone, that dissolves the claims of the Law in the most fundamental way imaginable—by charging it with unlocking the gates of sin.

Paul's quantum jump is thus rooted in his early life in Pharisaism. Yearning for eternal life and resurrection, he left no law unobserved. He appeared to himself and to others as having climbed, law by law, to heaven's gate. If anyone could be certain of sitting beside God the Father until the day of resurrection, surely it was Paul, who was "as to righteousness under the Law blameless." Little wonder, then, that when the disciples of Jesus trumpeted the good news of the resurrection, his anger was as fierce as his loyalty to the twofold Law was tenacious. If anyone persecuted the church violently, it was he. Yet it seems that all was not peaceful and tranquil in Paul's inner house. His blamelessness had deluded him into believing that his primordial impulses to sin had been dissolved when they had only been dammed up. His righteousness had misled him into believing that every nook and cranny, every fissure and crevice had been sealed off to sin. And yet there came a moment of blinding revelation when, it seems, his very blamelessness and his very righteousness goaded his primordial untamed impulses into a raging torrent pouring through the restraining dams of the Law and spilled Paul into the arms of the risen Christ, and he was reborn, truly saved, and determined to preach the true gospel of Christ's undemanding love, which dissolves and does not dam up the impulse to sin. Here were, at long last, the fruits of Paul's roots in Pharisaism.

IV

ANTI-SEMITISM IN THE NEW TESTAMENT

A paper delivered at a convocation of the Vatican Council's Nostra Aetate, 28 October 1965.
The Institute of Judaeo-Christian Studies, Setan Hall University (South Orange, NJ), 12 October 1980.

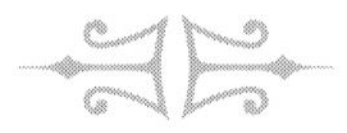

In addressing myself to this awesome question, fraught as it is with traps and pitfalls, I do so as a historian who is motivated primarily by a wish to know, to understand, and to make intelligible the past and as a Jew who firmly believes that since God is Truth, one is bound by this belief to distinguish as best one can between truth and falsehood, fact and fiction, intra-Jewish polemics and anti-Semitism. I am therefore focusing exclusively on the time-frame within which the events recorded in the New Testament were purported to have occurred and within which the Gospels, the Epistle of Paul, Acts, and the other books of the New Testament were written. I have made a special effort not to read back into the New Testament the anti-Semitism of late antiquity, the Middle Ages, and the modern period but to read the Gospels, the Epistles of Paul, Acts, and the other books of the New Testament as though I knew nothing of the anti-Semitic uses to which these writings were put in late antiquity, the Middle Ages, and modern times.

When, with these strictures in mind, one opens the New Testament, one is struck by the framework of Judaism that encloses all that is recorded in the Synoptic Gospels, Acts, and the Epistles of Paul. There is scarcely a page that does not have some proof-text drawn from the Old Testament: Abraham, Moses, David, and Elijah are the spiritual heroes; Jesus is a Jewish teacher who frequents the synagogue, visits the Temple, refutes the Sadducees, parries the Pharisees, evokes Scriptures, and ends his life on the cross under a *titulus* bearing the inscription Jesus, King of the Jews. Like Jesus, all his disciples are Jews because he seemed to them to be the Son of man, the Messiah, the scion of David, preaching the gospel of God's kingdom to the people of God. Paul, the most gifted preacher of the risen Christ, had been as to the Law a Pharisee, as to righteousness under the Law blameless. He had hounded and harassed the church for its blasphemous teaching that Jesus was the Christ and that he had risen from the dead. Yet when he saw Jesus resurrected and was impelled to preach the good news, it was the good news that God had revealed his son Jesus Christ so that impulse-ridden man would be able to overcome the power of sin. But this God was the God of Abraham and the God of Moses and the God of Israel. He was no new or alien God. He was the God of revelation who had just revealed through Jesus Christ the road to eternal life and resurrection. And one need not take Paul's word for this. One need but turn to Scriptures and there one would find the foreshadowings of Christ and that the true Israel would acknowledge and cling to Christ when he came.

Even the Gospel of John does not cut the umbilical cord completely. Its author still finds it necessary to cite scriptural proof-texts to confirm that Jesus must have been the Christ—proof-texts that the Jews stubbornly refused to acknowledge.

If, then, one reads these sources without any knowledge of how these texts were to be used at some future time, one would conclude that we have here a record of bitter religious controversy, exacerbated by the fact that the individual around whom the controversies centered had been subjected to a painful death, from which, according to his disciples, he had been resurrected. The parties to the controversy are at one another's throats over issues that would make sense only to those who were members of a community that shared the same basic ideas, concepts, and assumptions. God, revelation, Israel, prophetic visions, Messiah, resurrection—concepts so charged with sanctity and so fraught with life and death—could mean nothing to one who had not been nurtured in Judaism or one who had not been taught its doctrines. Indeed, even when it becomes obvious, as we read our sources, that non-Jews, Gentiles, have become very much a part of the movement, it is nonetheless evident that in the act of becoming a Christian there must have been some exposure to and adoption of such key concepts as God, Israel, Holy Scriptures, Messiah, and resurrection to sustain discourse within the community of Christians.

Now it is true that some very harsh acts are reported, some very harsh words are blurted out, and some very harsh feelings are expressed. But, the historian must ask, how could it have been otherwise? Following the death of Herod the Great and the decision of

Rome to rule Judea directly through procurators, the country was plunged into a tumult that refused to subside until after the Romans crushed the rebellion of the Jews in A.D. 70. There was hardly a day that went by without its distempers and hardly a week without its outbursts of violence. The Temple area was the scene of disruptive demonstrations, bloody battles between mobs of angry Jews and the soldiery. Assassinations were daily occurrences. The countryside was plagued by terrorist bands. Crucifixions were not infrequent and executions by other means a commonplace.

Confronted with a people gone "mad," the authorities were at a loss as to how to dampen the fires of discontent. The procurators had only limited options. Charged as they were by the emperors with the twofold task of collecting the tribute and maintaining law and order, they found themselves baffled and bewildered by this strange and alien people with their anomalous way of life, and with their stubborn adherence to their one God, and with their incomprehensible language. To govern such a people at all, the procurators had to have Jewish "eyes and ears" to keep them informed of where trouble was brewing and who the chief troublemakers might be.

Individuals with such "eyes and ears" were not hard to find. Herod himself had pointed the way. Frightened as he was of the threat to his power lurking in the Hasmonean high priesthood, Herod arrogated to himself the right both to appoint the high priest and to dismiss him at will. Furthermore, to underscore the high priest's total dependence on Herod's goodwill, Herod had the holy vestments of the high priest placed under lock and key, releasing them to the high priest only a few days prior to the festivals. The high priest had thus already been fashioned by Herod into a political instrument prior to the takeover of political responsibility for Judea by Coponius, the first of the Roman procurators.

High priests appointed by and totally dependent for their tenure on the whim of the procurators had a high incentive to see with the eyes of a procurator and to hear with his ears. Yet not every high priest had eyes piercing enough or ears finely tuned enough to satisfy the procurators. Hence the tenure of most high priests proved to be short and swift, a tenure numbered in weeks and months, not in years. No high priest therefore could have had any illusions as to the risks he was taking when he accepted the high priestly office from the hands of a procurator. He knew with absolute certainty that if his eyes blurred or his ears dulled, he would be unceremoniously dismissed.

The high priest was thus strictly a political instrument. He served exclusively the interests of Rome. His job was to make the procurator's twofold task easier by urging the people to pay the tribute and by helping the procurator maintain law and order. The high priest was not primarily a religious functionary but a religious figurehead who held the sacred office only so long as the procurator was pleased with his "political," not religious, performance.

To carry out his political mandate effectively, the high priest had to have the cooperation of other influential individuals who, like the high priest, also had a stake in maintaining law and order. From among these individuals, the high priest would select his privy council, a sanhedrin, which he would convoke from time to time whenever he felt he needed their judgment as to whether a dissident or troublemaker should be brought to the attention of the procurator. Such individuals functioned not in a religious but in a political capacity, since the high priest's privy council, the sanhedrin, was an extension of the high priest's role as the eyes and ears of the procurator. Hence a judgment would be made on political, not religious, grounds, even if the troublemaker or dissident was himself a religious charismatic or advocated revolutionary violence with an appeal to religious beliefs and sensibilities. Thus both Sadducees and Pharisees could sit in the high priest's sanhedrin and pass judgment on a dissident or troublemaker—a collaboration between two such fundamentally different groupings that would otherwise have been impossible. For when it came to religious law, the Sadducees totally rejected the Oral Law of the Pharisees, while the Pharisees rejected the claim of the Sadducees that God had given one Law, the Written Law, on Sinai and not two Laws. The Sadducees looked upon the Pharisees as unredeemed heretics, while the Pharisees reciprocated in kind.

Collaboration between Sadducees and Pharisees on political issues, however, at this point in time was possible because both the Sadducees and Pharisees had long since come to recognize that a sharp line of demarcation had to be drawn separating the domain of political sovereignty from the domain of religious sovereignty. It was the only realistic way to avoid the kind of bitter and bloody civil war that had flared up for a full generation when Alexander Janneus sought to repress the Pharisees by force and to impose the onefold Law of the Sadducees on the entire people. Impelled by the logic inherent in these tragic events, both the Sadducees and Pharisees adopted the doctrine of the two realms, the one political-secular and the other religious, a doctrine that proclaimed that so long as the political-secular authority respected the autonomy of the religious realm, the Sadducees and Pharisees would recognize that the political-secular authority exercised sovereignty in its realm with divine sanction. This doctrine, which had been operative throughout Herod's reign, was confirmed when both the Sadducees and Pharisees proclaimed that the Romans had a right to exact tribute so long as they did not encroach upon the religious domain. By reaffirming the doctrine of the two realms, the Sadducees and Pharisees were positioned to join together with a politically appointed high priest to uphold this doctrine, a doctrine that, it seemed to them, was vital to uphold if the Jews were not to be plunged into suicidal revolt against Rome.

The Sadducees and Pharisees could also collaborate on this doctrine because they had adopted toward one another a policy of live and let live. This policy likewise was a lesson derived from the experience of the civil war during the reign of Alexander Janneus, when both the Sadducees and Pharisees had struggled violently for supremacy over the Law. Both groups agreed to live and let live. So long as a Sadducean high priest performed his duties in the Temple in accordance with the Oral Laws, the *Halachot* of the Pharisees, the Pharisees agreed not to challenge his right to be high priest. Likewise, so long as the calendar that regulated the festivals was the Pharisaic calendar and so long as all public religious functions when carried out by Sadducean functionaries were in accordance with Pharisaic prescriptions, the Pharisees would make no effort to subject the Sadducees to Pharisaic law or hail them before Pharisaic courts. No restrictions, however, were placed on ideological controversy. Both Pharisees and Sadducees could let mocking and destructive words fly and could toss barbed proof-texts at each other as spirited onlookers egged them on. But that is as far as these fundamental differences were allowed to go.

There was one singular difference, however, between the role of the high priest and those who participated in the high priest's sanhedrin. The high priest was high priest because of his own ambitions to hold high office. Otherwise he would have no interest in accepting a position so dependent on the whim of the procurator. His tenure as high priest, after all, depended on his active ferreting out of dissenters and revolutionaries. By contrast, those who agreed to serve on the high priest's sanhedrin did so out of the fear that dissenters and troublemakers might, by their recklessness, bring down the wrath of Rome on all the Jews. Unlike the high priest, they held no high office on Roman sufferance, nor did they reap any personal advantage from serving on the high priest's sanhedrin. For many of them, it was indeed a distasteful responsibility, one that they undertook only because they did not know how else to cope with the rash of dissidence, distemper, and violence that at any moment could provoke a savage remedy from the Romans. To serve on the high priest's sanhedrin was a thankless task as well because it exposed one to the charge of aiding and abetting Roman rule and participating in the shedding of innocent blood.

The Sadducees and Pharisees—and the Essenes as well—had thus been pressed by the pummelings of experience into a mosaic of Judaisms. However unbridgeable the gap dividing Sadducees from Pharisees and Essenes may have been, they all three appeared in the eyes of the political authorities, whether they were emperors, governors, procurators, or puppet kings, as a unity of distinguishable hues, colors, and shapes rather than as a batch of noncohering entities. For though each of these forms of Judaism was fundamentally incompatible one with the other and although their beliefs and claims were nonnegotiable, they were nonetheless unified in their commitment to the doctrine of the two realms and to the policy of live and let live.

This mosaic of Judaisms presented no real problem for the Romans because the line of demarcation separating Caesar's turf from God's was relatively sharp and clear. So long as emperor, governor, high priest, and puppet king did not flaunt the icons of the emperor in Judea and so long as they did not insist on setting up the bust of the emperor in the Temple, Jews were duty-bound to pay the tribute and maintain the peace. Contrapuntally, so long as the daily sacrifice for the life and health of the emperor was offered in the Temple and so long as Roman legitimacy was not challenged on religious grounds, the Roman authorities agreed to respect the religious autonomy of the mosaic of Judaisms. When, in fact, this line was crossed on two occasions by the Romans—one time by Pontius Pilate and another time by Gaius Caligula—the Jews as a body refused to obey and bared their necks to the Roman sword rather than allow Pontius Pilate to parade the Roman standards with the image of the emperor through Jerusalem and rather than acquiesce in Caligula's demand that his bust be set up in the Temple. In each instance, the Romans backed away from butchering an entire people.

The line of demarcation was clear enough, but there existed blurred lines as well. What were the authorities to do if these blurred lines were crossed? When, for example, two fanatical disciples of Judas and Matthias pulled down the golden eagle that Herod had erected on the Temple as a symbol of loyalty to Rome, were these fanatics merely seeking to rectify a violation of religious autonomy or were they masking a political act with the trappings of religious ideology? Did God forbid the making of representations of living creatures under all circumstances or only if these representations might become objects of worship? After all, God himself had commanded Moses to have cherubim fashioned to uphold the Ark of the Covenant in the Tabernacle. Was then the golden eagle a symbol of loyalty or an object of worship? Herod, who regarded the golden eagle as a symbol of loyalty, was outraged at this act and ordered the perpetrators to be put to death. Yet Josephus, who was an ardent adherent to the doctrine of the two realms, nonetheless thought that Herod had been unnecessarily provocative, since he failed to take into account the religious sensitivities of the Jews to any images in the Temple area that were not specifically commanded by God. Far from stilling the disquietude, Herod's execution of the fanatics led to mass demonstrations, riots, and a heavy loss of lives when a few days after his death all hell broke loose in the Temple area.

This was one kind of blurring of lines. But there was another kind of blurring that is of especial interest to us. This was the blurring that enveloped the status of charismatic and prophetlike individuals who began to raise their voices in the no-man's-land separating God's turf from Caesar's. For no sooner had Herod died and no sooner had Rome decided to rule the Jews in a more direct fashion, then there arose outside the mosaic of Judaisms new forms that did not bind themselves to the doctrine of the two realms. One of these forms, which Josephus calls the Fourth Philosophy, was clear and unequivocal in its revolutionary goals. The tribute, they proclaimed, must not be paid for to pay it was to acknowledge that Caesar and not God was lord and master. God alone was to be called Lord and Master; God alone was *the* Emperor. To acknowledge Roman sovereignty was tantamount to disacknowledging God's.

But no such clear-cut message was forthcoming from the charismatics and the prophets. Since these charismatics and prophets preached as the spirit moved them, they did not speak with one voice. Some may have been blatantly anti-Caesar, some may have been more muted, and some spoke in multiple tongues. One such charismatic was John the Baptist.

John the Baptist, according to Josephus, was a goodly man who called upon the people to repent, live righteous lives, practice justice, and confirm their resolution through baptism. Josephus's vignette of John is fleshed out in the Gospel of Mark where John not only calls on the people to repent but he also links their repentance to the coming of the kingdom of God. What, then, of these teachings of John? Were they to be denounced as subversive or praised as exemplary? Was his proclamation of the imminence of the kingdom the anticipation of a visionary or was it a veiled threat to Roman rule? As far as Josephus was concerned, John was an exemplary figure. His call for repentance, for righteousness, and for justice was merely echoing the voice of the prophets of old and was therefore worthy of being heeded. For Josephus, John was a religious teacher and not a subversive. Rome had nothing to fear from so benign and apolitical a charismatic.

Yet Herod the Tetrarch did not agree with Josephus. He was concerned not so much with what John preached as with the crowds who were moved by John's eloquence. It was the crowds, not John, who were frightening. Crowds could get out of hand, erupt in violence, and pay no heed to a charismatic's plea that this is not what he had meant at all. Compelled to make a decision one way or another, Herod the Tetrarch, with vivid memories of the thousands whom Archelaus had been forced to slay on the Temple Mount, decided to err on the side of rigor and ordered John to be put to death.

A similar fate befell Theudas, who does not seem to have called for a revolt against Rome but only prophesied that God would split the Jordan for his people once again. But, like John, he attracted crowds, and crowds were dangerous.

And one final instance of how murky this no-man's-land could be. It involved the execution of James, the brother of Jesus. James, so Josephus tells us, was arrested by the high priest Ananus and brought before a sanhedrin that Ananus had convoked, which ordered him stoned to death. This high-handedness of Ananus so enraged those whom Josephus refers to as the most accurate observers of the laws, i.e., the Pharisees, that they reported Ananus's illegal act—he had convoked a sanhedrin on his own authority at a time when the procurator was out of the city—to both Agrippa II and the procurator. Both in turn were so furious that Ananus was removed from the high priesthood after having served only two months in this post.

What are we to make of this happening? Clearly neither Josephus nor the Pharisees were convinced that the teachings of James were so politically dangerous that the high priest Ananus could have been justified in acting in so high-handed a manner. Indeed, by implication, James's teachings were deemed so apolitical that had the procurator been in Jerusalem and had James been arrested and tried by a sanhedrin and an adverse judgment reached, then as likely as not the procurator would have reversed the judgment and released James from custody.

What becomes more and more clear as we read Josephus is that Judea had become ungovernable. Neither heavy-handedness nor light-handedness seemed to work. Heavy-handedness only made the dissidents and revolutionaries more bitter and set the people's teeth on edge, while light-handedness was as often as not taken as a sign of weakness. The authorities were especially bewildered and baffled by the charismatics and prophets, by the John the Baptists and the Theudases. Were their preachings mere echoings of the prophets or were they tinged with subversion?

Were the crowds attracted to these charismatic prophets harmless gatherings of penitents or of highly combustible dissidents? The authorities did not know how to answer these questions any more than authorities have ever been able to answer questions such as these when a society is on the brink of revolution. For we must not for one moment forget that precisely because the authorities had no answers and precisely because Judea had become ungovernable, the Jews finally threw all caution to the wind and rose up in a rebellion against Rome, a rebellion that was doomed from the outset to undergo a crushing and tragic defeat.

Jesus was born into this matrix of dissidence, disorientation, and violence and his ministry was carried out among people wracked with pain, badgered by despair, and baffled by events they could not understand. And it was Jesus' destiny to have preached his gospel of repentance and the coming of the kingdom of God during those years when Pontius Pilate was procurator and Caiaphas was high priest. This was fraught with tragedy. For Pontius Pilate, as limned by Josephus, was not only harsh but provocative. He was the only procurator who, on his own authority, ordered that the standards of the emperor be flaunted through the streets of Jerusalem in audacious defiance of the doctrine of the two realms. He, too, was the procurator who infuriated the people by robbing the Temple treasury for funds to build an aqueduct. He was also a procurator who used agents provocateurs to mingle with the crowds to stir them up so that they could be easily beaten down by the soldiery.

Caiaphas, too, was no ordinary high priest. He had distinguished himself above all others by holding on to his office longer than any other high priest. Indeed, Caiaphas proved to have such good eyes and ears that when Pontius Pilate was appointed procurator, he was so impressed with Caiaphas's record that he confirmed him as high priest. This, coupled with the fact that Caiaphas remained high priest during the entire tenure of Pontius Pilate as procurator, gives us some measure of Caiaphas's loyalty and dependability. If ever there was a high priest who saw with the eyes of a procurator and heard with the ears of a procurator, it was Caiaphas. It was therefore inevitable that when the news of a charismatic called Jesus—who was preaching repentance *and* the coming of the kingdom of God; was being talked of as the Son of man, the Messiah, the scion of David; and was drawing crowds and causing a rumpus in the Temple area—reached the ears of Caiaphas, he would move swiftly, subtly, and decisively to cut this Jesus down before the crowds got out of hand and required the calling out of the soldiery.

It was all then very much the way it is reported in the Gospels. Jesus was a charismatic; he was believed by his followers to be the Son of man, the Messiah, the scion of David who would usher in the kingdom of God; his preachings attracted crowds; his overthrowing of the tables of the money chargers in the Temple set off a disturbance in the Temple area. He thus was bound to be frightening to the high priest, who was not interested in whether Jesus' teachings were or were not apolitical. All that he was interested in was that here was a charismatic, like John, whose eloquence was attracting crowds and who was preaching to them of the coming of the kingdom of God, a kingdom in which the Jews would not be ruled by the Roman emperor, or his procurator, or his high priest. For Caiaphas this was treason enough. And when to this treason was added the fact that Caiaphas had no way of knowing for certain that even if Jesus was a naive visionary, totally apolitical, and utterly opposed to violence, Jesus would be able to control crowds once they were stirred by the certainty that the kingdom of God must indeed be at hand and that Jesus was the Son of man, the Messiah, the scion of David, who was ushering this kingdom in.

Caiaphas, faced as he was with a John the Baptist conundrum, solved it even as Herod the Tetrarch had decided his own with John the Baptist: Better to err on the side of rigor than to take chances on the side of permissiveness. Jesus was therefore arrested and brought before a sanhedrin convoked by the high priest to determine whether or not the claims being made by Jesus himself or claims that were being made about him by his followers were claims that could have dangerous political consequences. The claims themselves may have been expressed exclusively in religious terminology and may have been articulated exclusively in religious imagery, but they were evaluated by the high priest and the council exclusively within the framework of their potential political consequences. Nor could this be otherwise. A sanhedrin convoked by the high priest was not a *boulé*, the Greek term used in Josephus's day for the *bet din*, the senate, of the Scribes-Pharisees, but a council convoked by the high priest to help him deal with issues of law and order. The question was therefore simple and it was political: Was the claim that Jesus was the King of the Jews likely to provoke disorder or not? The high priest and the council decided that it was indeed a dangerous claim, however couched it might be in religious terminology and however alien the notion of revolutionary violence may have been to Jesus himself.

Having been found dangerous, Jesus was turned over to Pontius Pilate, who likewise had to decide the issue on political, not religious, grounds. The inscription over the cross, King of the Jews, could leave no doubt in the minds of those who read it that Pontius Pilate had concluded that Jesus was politically dangerous.

We thus have in the Gospels the tragic fate of a charismatic who, like John, was religiously motivated and, like John, attracted crowds of avid listeners with his eloquence and charisma—and crowds were dangerous. The high priest did what he did because he wanted to continue in his post as high priest. The members of the sanhedrin did what they did because they were frightened of the bloodbath that might follow an outbreak sparked by shouts of "Long live David, King of the Jews," "Long live Jesus, the Messiah," "Long live Jesus, King of the Jews." Pontius Pilate did what he did because the Roman emperor had charged him with the responsibility of collecting the tribute and maintaining law and order. Everyone thus did what he did because no one knew what else could be done. Dissidence, tumult, violence, and the cacophonous cries of charismatics and prophets so blurred the vision and so deafened the ears that whatever one did was wrong.

But such a dispassionate appeal to the logic of desperation would have been incomprehensible to Jesus' disciples and followers if such an appeal had been possible. All that they knew is what they saw and what they heard and what they imagined. And that which they had seen and heard was that their beloved Teacher and Master—the Son of man and Messiah in whom they had believed and put their trust—had been arrested by the high priest, tried before a sanhedrin, and turned over to Pontius Pilate, who had him crucified. And that which they imagined were the charges that must have been brought against him. They were therefore stunned, grief-stricken, and angry. Some of their fellow Jews had been party to the arrest, trial, and crucifixion of their Teacher and Master, and these Jews were deserving of all the venom that grief and sorrow and anger could spew forth. But it was the venom of Jews who, like their fellow Jews, believed that the one and only God had given his Torah to his people Israel and had promised through his prophets that he would some day restore to Israel her former glory. And they also believed with the Pharisees that God would grant eternal life to the soul of every individual who obeyed God's Law and resurrection to his body. Indeed, so total was their belief in eternal life and resurrection that they saw Jesus risen from the dead and greeted him as the living Christ.

We are thus dealing with Jewish venom, not anti-Semitism. The disciples of Jesus were angry at their fellow Jews for failing to recognize who Jesus was when he was alive and who he was after he had risen from the dead. They hurled proof-texts at their Jewish opponents, not from Plato or Aristotle or the sacred literature of the mystery cults but from the Pentateuch and the Prophets and the Hagiographa. They confronted the Pharisees with the very belief in the resurrection of the dead that the Pharisees themselves had preached to the people. They likewise followed in the footsteps of the Pharisees when they began to preach the gospel of the risen Christ to the Gentiles. For did not the Pharisees themselves preach their gospel to the Gentiles and did they not welcome sincere proselytes and regard them as more loyal sons of Israel than the Sadducees who rejected the twofold Law, denied the resurrection, and were doomed, so the Pharisees believed, to a life of eternal suffering beyond the grave?

There was thus no love lost between those who proclaimed Christ to be the fulfillment of Scripture and those who rejected such proclamations as absurd and blasphemous. The Pharisees were especially enraged because in so many ways Jesus' teachings had squared with their own and because the disciples of Jesus, like their Teacher, frequented the synagogue, the house of worship of the Pharisees. The Scribes-Pharisees were thus afraid that the preaching of the gospel of the risen Christ might gain adherents precisely because they themselves had been responsible for making Jesus' resurrection credible. After all, was not this belief a hallmark of Pharisaism? Resurrection was not absurd; it was what salvation was all about. It is not surprising, therefore, that the Pharisees expelled the disciples and adherents of Jesus from the synagogue—an expulsion that was resisted, resented, and denounced by the Jewish Christians, who continued to affirm their loyalty to the Scribes-Pharisees even after they were expelled. "The Scribes and Pharisees sit in Moses' seat," the author of Matthew has Jesus reassure his listeners. "So you must do all that they tell you to"—even though they are hypocrites, whitewashed tombs, and venemous vipers. It thus turns out that the most bitter denunciation of the Scribes-Pharisees in all the New Testament (Matthew 23), where they are accused of harassing the Jewish Christians, is in the very chapter in which Jesus himself insists that no matter what the provocation, the umbilical cord tying the Christians to the Scribes-Pharisees may not be severed.

This persecution and harassment of the Christians is most strikingly driven home by Paul when, in Philippians 3:5–6, he tells us that when he was "as to the Law a Pharisee "and" as to righteousness under the Law blameless," he was "as to zeal a persecutor of the church (Philippians 3:6). Paul is even more vehement in his Epistle to the Galatians (1:13): "For you have heard, " he reminds the Galatians, "of my former life in Judaism, how I persecuted the church of God violently and tried to destroy it."

We thus have reason enough for the hostility that enflamed the Pharisees on the one hand and the early Christians on the other. The Pharisees were outraged by Jesus' defiance of their religious authority when he was alive, and they were even more outraged when, after his crucifixion, his followers proclaimed that Jesus the Christ had risen from the dead. They therefore expelled the Christians from the synagogues. The Christians, in turn, were outraged that the Pharisees should have rejected the Son of man, the Messiah who had proved that he was the Christ by his resurrection. They were bitter at the Scribes-Pharisees for having been party to the crucifixion of Jesus by the participation of some of them in the sanhedrin that the high priest had convoked. That the sanhedrin that tried Jesus was a political body, convoked by a high priest appointed by the procurator, and that the Scribes-Pharisees who sat in this council were judging Jesus on political, not religious, grounds were for them irrelevant. Jesus' disciples were simple and unsophisticated devotees of a charismatic preacher who had no interest in or understanding of the political dangers lurking in their Master's preachings and his charisma. All that they knew was that their precious, gentle, and loving Teacher had been crucified. And then, when it dawned upon them that he had risen from the dead and they had proclaimed the good news that Jesus had been resurrected and therefore he must be the Christ, they were stunned by the repression that followed after their proclamation of this good news. *So the Pharisees were outraged and angry, and the Christians were outraged and angry.* But since it was the Christians who preserved the anger of both sides, first in oral transmission and then in a written canon of sacred books, it is the New Testament and not the Mishnah or the Tosefta that is the repository of the harshness of feeling that stirred both camps of Jews.

For what we have preserved in the Gospels and in the Epistles of Paul is the record of a struggle for the soul of Judaism, a struggle that was reminiscent of the struggle for this soul during the reign of Alexander Janneus. For a generation the followers of the Pharisees fought not merely with words but with weapons of violence against Alexander Janneus and his Sadducean supporters. So fierce was this religious civil war that Alexander Janneus crucified not one but hundreds of rebels in a public ceremony, while the Pharisees for their part retaliated by having Diogenes and other advisers of Alexander executed when they regained some of their power and influence during the reign of Salome Alexandra.

This murderous conflict clearly had nothing to do with anti-Semitism. It revolved instead around the issues of whether God had given one Law or two; whether a scholar class, not even mentioned in the Pentateuch, had the right to sit in Moses' seat; whether a *Kenesset Hagedolah*, a Great Synagogue, though nowhere authorized in the Pentateuch, had the right to appoint to the high priesthood a priest who was not of the family of Zadok; whether rewards and punishments were to be meted out in this world or in the world to come; whether membership in the people of Israel was preeminently that of the flesh or of the spirit. The hostility that these differences brewed were as searing as any hostility that the differences between the early Chrisitians and the Pharisees brewed. Indeed these differences were even more polarizing, since they embroiled the Sadducees and Pharisees in a generation-long civil war.

Then why, we may ask, has the hostility reported in the Gospels been attributed to anti-Semitism when here, too, the issues revolved around strictly intrareligious concerns, such as whether or not Jesus was the Son of man or the Messiah; or whether the kingdom of God was close at hand or not; or whether the Traditions of the Elders were sacrosanct or not; or whether Jesus had risen from the dead or not; or whether membership in the people of Israel derived from the flesh or not, and if not from the flesh but from the spirit, would not Gentiles have a claim to being Israelites that was more powerful than the claim of those who were born into Israel but had rejected Jesus?

Here, then, it seems to me is the nub of the problem. Since the overwhelming majority of the Jews rejected the gospel of the risen Christ and since the Christian churches more and more consisted of Christians who had been Gentiles, not Jews, the issues that had in the beginning been intrareligious issues affecting Jews became more and more interreligious issues that faced both Jews and gentile Christians. What had happened was that the distinction that the Pharisees had made between Israel of the flesh (the Sadducees) and Israel of the spirit (the Pharisees), a distinction that had energized them to traverse land and sea to gain proselytes, this distinction when taken up by Paul and by John had consequences utterly different from those consequences that such a distinction had had for the Pharisees. For whereas the proselytes gained by the Pharisees represented only a small fraction of Jews following the Pharisees, the gentile proselytes gained by Paul and the gentile Christians of John's community had come to represent the overwhelming majority of Christians, first in Paul's churches and subsequently in all churches, as the Gospel of John presupposes. It was not surprising, therefore, that such Christians, *never having been Jews* and having had no contact with Jewish Christians other then through their readings of the Synoptics, Acts, and the Epistles of Paul *came to look upon the Jews as outsiders.* Hence the issues that had been at one time intra-Jewish issues—Son of man, Son of God, Messiah, resurrection—became interreligious issues between Jews and gentile Christians.

There was now a Christian entity and a Jewish entity squared for battle, as the Gospel of John bears witness. For whereas the Synoptic Gospels reveal for us a historical Jesus who is eminently human and concerned overwhelmingly with ministering to his fellow Jews, the Gospel of John reveals to us a Jesus who is eminently divine, whose light is unable to penetrate the blindness of the Jews who knew him not even though he was, in his humanity, one of them. Hence what Jesus said and did while he was alive was significant only to the degree that it reflected or foreshadowed his divine and not his human nature. John's portrait of Jesus is of a divine being who has been selected to refract the divinity that was beaming out from the light that was temporarily housed within him.

The Fourth Gospel is thus a very different kind of gospel. Unlike Mark, John does not begin his gospel with a prophetic proclamation, nor does he focus on Jesus' genealogy, as does Matthew, or on the factual reliability of his gospel, as does Luke. Instead, John begins with an outright affirmation that Jesus was not really a man at all, however human he appeared to be, but the Word/Logos-God and the God-Logos who was the Light and the Life. Yet though his divinity should have been evident through his humanity, it was not recognized by the Jews even though he had come to them, his very kith and kin, humanly speaking. Instead of being illuminated by the Divine Light, the Jews actively sought to have him crucified, even though Pontius Pilate had sought to keep him alive. By actively participating in the crucifixion of Jesus, they had forfeited their right to be the people of God. They had doubly forfeited their right when after his crucifixion they had stubbornly refused to see him as resurrected.

By contrast, the Gentiles had recognized Jesus' divinity. They had seen him risen from the dead. As seers and believers, they had earned the right to be called the people of God, a right that the Jews had forfeited by virtue of their unseeing and their unbelieving. It was the Jews, according to John, who had rejected God even though God had sent Jesus to them, aglow with Divine Light. It was the Gentiles who had embraced him even though in his humanity he had not been one of them. Hence the people of God can no longer be the Jews but the Gentiles.

Is then the Gospel of John anti-Semitic, or is it an intra-religious polemic? Is the Gospel of John manipulating the life, ministry, and crucifixion of Jesus to arouse hostility against an innocent people, as was to be the case in late antiquity, the Middle Ages, and modern times, or was it meant to deliver the coup de grace to the continued insistence on the part of the Jews that they and not the Christians were the people of God? If it were factually true that Jesus had been tried and crucified as reported in the Synoptic Gospels, and if indeed it were true that most Jews had refused to believe in Jesus' resurrection, and if it were no less true that most Christians in John's day were gentile Christians and believed that Jesus had indeed been God incarnate, then from the point of view of such Christians, the Jews had indeed been blind to Jesus' divinity when he was alive and had remained blind to his divinity even after he had been resurrected. Hence if Jesus had been crucified and the Jews had played some role in this crucifixion, then Christians such as these would truly believe that the Jews had crucified God and in so doing had forfeited their right to be the people of God.

As a historian who has spent a lifetime seeking to understand the interaction of the religious realm with the human realm and who has been especially concerned with the how and the why of anti-Semitism, I must conclude that however much the Gospel of John lent itself to anti-Semitic uses in later times, it cannot be considered anti-Semitic within its historical frame unless we are willing to apply the same measure to other intrareligious controversies. Did Josephus deride polytheism because he was anti-Thucydides, or anti-Plato, or anti-Stoic? Or did he mock polytheism because he considered its claims to be patently false? Did Jews and Muslims or Christians and Muslims tangle with each other because the former were anti-Arab or anti-Persian or because the latter espoused what Jews and Christians believed to be false teachings about God and his revelations? It is sad indeed that intrareligious and interreligious controversies mar the history of even the most liberating religions, but there is a difference between interreligious controversy that is sincerely generated, however unseemly, and the phenomenon of anti-Semitism, which, in my book, is a *deliberate manipulation of sacred texts to cause harm to the Jews so as to solve economic, social, political, and ecclesiastical problems.*

What we have in the Synoptics is an outcry of grief, resentment, disappointment, and hatred on the part of the followers of Jews toward all those who they believed had been in one way or another party to Jesus' crucifixion and toward all those who had rejected the gospel of the risen Christ. These were harsh times, which made for harsh actions, harsh judgments, and harsh words. And what we have in John is an intrareligious polemic seeking to strike a mortal blow at Jewish claims to still be the people of God despite their rejection of Jesus Christ.

A tragic skein is thus woven into the tapestry of Christian origins—a skein woven into the warp and woof of the process by which one religious movement separates and differentiates itself from another. It is clearly visible in the struggle of the Pharisees to displace the Sadducees; the Karaites to displace the Rabbanites; the anti-Maimonists to displace the Maimonists; the Chasidim to displace the Mitnagdim; the Reformers to displace the Orthodox; and the secular Jewish nationalists to displace the religionists.

This skein is no less vivid in the struggles that have marked the rise, consolidation, and spread of Christianity: Paul excoriates those who preached false and misleading gospels; the Roman Catholic and the Greek Orthodox churches went their separate ways; Luther called down fire and brimstone on the Pope and all his minions and opened the sluice gates to decades of religious wars; Puritans rose up in violent revolt against Anglicans and were themselves confronted with fissures in their own ranks. Sometimes these fissures energized only violent words and harsh accusations; but at other times they energized murderous conflict. But whether confined to a clash of words or expanded into a clash of arms, no separation was ever calm, peaceful or serene. A religious body, whether Jewish, Christian, or Muslim, cannot be dismembered without wracking pain and violent convulsions. This pain and violence are indelibly etched in the harsh words and the harsh deeds that were twisted out of the pain and the anguish of separation and differentiation.

But there is one other skein that is also woven alongside the skein of tragedy. That skein is the skein of reconciliation. No matter how harsh the words and the deeds, no matter how sacred and immutable the texts, no matter how indelibly etched the pain and the anguish, there always has come a time when the spirit of reconciliation begins to fill the hearts and minds of even the most stalwart protagonists and there is a diminution of hatred, a surcease of violence, and even a touch of love. The Pharisees and Sadducees abandoned murderous strife for a policy of live and let live; the Rabbanites and Karaites settled for coexistence; the Maimonists and anti-Maimonists discovered the art of compromise; the Chasidim and Mitnagdim discovered that God had prepared a table where former enemies could break bread as friends; Reform, Conservative, and Orthodox Jews found that trudging parallel paths avoided snarled intersections; and secular and nationalist Jews and religionists concluded that rendering unto Caesar what was Caesar's and unto God what was God's was, after all, a workable formula.

This skein of reconciliation likewise weaves in and out of the tapestry of Christianity. The Christian canon preserves Paul alongside Acts; Matthew alongside Luke; John alongside the Synoptics; the Epistle of Romans alongside Timothy. The Roman and Byzantine churches adopted a policy of live and let live. The violent upheavals that pitted Catholics and Protestants against each other finally quieted down, and ways and means were found that allowed for peaceful coexistence.

But the skein of reconciliation is not only to be seen in the tapestry of Judaism and in the tapestry of Christianity, but also in the tapestry of Judeo-Christianity. Although there came a time when Christianity had become unhinged from Judaism and when the hostile texts in the New Testament had indeed become lethal and destructive weapons aimed at the destruction of Judaism and the humiliation and degradation of the Jewish people, there came other times when the sword was sheathed and the hostile texts were allowed to lie dormant. Hostility toward the Jews waxed and waned in intensity. From the ninth till the thirteenth centuries, the Jews living in the Holy Roman Empire, in France, and in England were a privileged class and not at all a parish people. In the thirteenth century when their fortunes waned in northern Europe, Jews flourished under benign Christian monarchs in Aragon and Castille. In the fifteenth century when their lives were made miserable in Christian Spain, Jews found welcoming havens in Renaissance Italy and Christian Poland. In the seventeenth century when they were ghettoized in Italy and pogrommed in Poland, they found doors opening for them in Protestant Holland, England, and the colonies of North America. And from the eighteenth century on, Jews have coexisted as a small minority among Christians of every stripe in the United States. Yet these times of relatively peaceful coexistence—a coexistence that from time to time was marked by mutual respect and appreciation—were not sparked off by denuding the New Testament of those proof-texts that had been drawn upon to deprive the Jews of their legal rights, to strip them of their wealth, to pogrom their communities and sack their synogogues, and to expel them from lands in which Christian princes and Christian prelates had urged them to settle. Long before our enlightened age and long before toleration had become a precious value, Christian rulers and churchmen had, at certain times and under certain circumstances, desisted from using the New Testament as an arsenal of lethal proof-texts to humiliate, degrade, pauperize, pogrom, and expel the Jews.

"At certain times and under certain circumstances"—these are the key to our understanding of this phenomenon. Whenever Christian societies were enjoying overall well-being and whenever these societies were expanding in such a way that opportunities were widening for all, Jews found themselves welcome and endowed with impressive rights and privileges. During times such as these, the hostile texts in the New Testament were allowed to lie relatively dormant. Contrariwise, whenever Christian societies were distintegrating and suffering constrictions, the hostile texts in the New Testament were reactivated and utilized in telling and destructive ways.

The problem, then, is not primarily the New Testament but the spirit that moves us. If our spirit is hostile, then the New Testament will feed our hostility. If, on the other hand, our spirit is benign, the hostile texts will lose their sting and our attention will be focused on the texts that are redolent with love, compassion, and charity.

Since, then, both Judaism and Christianity are threaded by these two skeins—tragic conflict on the one hand and reconciliation on the other—each of these umbilically linked religions leaves us the choice of the one or the other. If we choose the spirit of tragic conflict, then the harsh words in the Gospels, Acts, the Epistles of Paul, and the other books of the New Testament will come alive again with all the hatred and the venom that was spewed out during the pain and anguish of separation. If this choice is made, then the New Testament will serve as the *textus classicus* for anti-Semitism. The question will be Who crucified Jesus? and the answer forthcoming from the proof-texts will be the Jews.

If, on the other hand, we are moved by the spirit of reconciliation, we will be moved to frame the question in a radically new way. We will ask not *Who* crucified Jesus? but *What* crucified

Jesus? By asking What rather than Who, we dramatize that the crucifixion took place within a framework of harshness, violence, and tumult and in a society that defied governance. Emperors, governors, and high priests—all were baffled, bewildered, and helpless. The teeth of all Jews were set on edge. Little wonder, then, that there was clawing and biting and the spewing of venom. It was not who one was but where in this convulsing framework one happened to be. Like a Greek tragedy, everyone's script was prewritten, everyone's fate preordained. What crucified Jesus? The Roman imperial system, of course. It was a system that pummeled and shattered the Jews and literally drove them out of their minds so that they did not know what they were doing.

If, however, we choose the spirit of reconciliation, we will read the Gospels, Acts, and the other books of the New Testament as an account of a human and not a divine tragedy. As human beings, Jews and non-Jews of every stripe behaved in a human way—with fear, pain, bitterness and resentment—however much they may have felt the touch and the love of God. As a human tragedy, the New Testament is not anti-Semitic. It is a record of perceptions perceived, feelings felt, and conclusions drawn by participants in an awesome tragedy. As such, the bitterness, hatred, and harshness that it records are essentially no different than the bitterness, hatred, and harshness that have accompanied the dismemberment of religious bodies, be they Jewish, Christian, Muslim, or what have you. The New Testament reveals how very hard it is for human beings to be divine, and it is not a revelation of God's rejection of the Jews for all time and his wish to continually seek their hurt. Texts filled with hostility will thus be read as time-bound and human-bound. But as for those texts that tell us of God's gentle love and compassion and of Christ's loving outreach to every one of us, they are not time-bound, place-bound, or human-bound but divine-bound. Once this distinction is made, we will read the New Testament on one level as the record of human beings entrapped in the realm of the What and on another level as the record of God's effort to lift human beings out of the realm of the tragically human into the realm of the serenely divine.

With these options lying before us, we are free to choose between the spirit of hostility and the spirit of conciliation. *The New Testament cannot choose for us.* It will become whatever the spirit of our choice moves it to become. Dangled on the edge of such a choice, do we gathered here really have a choice? Has not our spirit of reconciliation already made the choice for us? Shall we not, then, Jews and Christians alike, render unto the human condition what is human in the New Testament and render unto God what is divine therein?

V

A JEW LOOKS AT THE NEW TESTAMENT

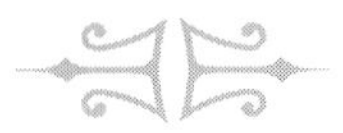

As the title of my paper "A Jew Looks at the New Testament" suggests, the views that I share with you this morning are the views of a single Jew. They are not the views of either the Jewish people as a whole or any fraction thereof. For all I know, these views may be singular, shared by no other Jew. They are nonetheless the views of a Jew who is deeply committed to Judaism and who has for more than a generation been teaching the history of Jews and Judaism to rabbinic students at the Hebrew Union College and to Christian graduate students as well. Nonetheless, what I shall share with you is the outcome of a highly personal odyssey that reaches back to my early life in Judaism when I was as to the Law a Pharisee, as to righteousness under the Law blameless, and as to the writings of the New Testament both ignorant and rejective; and that extends to this very moment when I stand before you unbound by the Law, highly insecure as to my righteousness, knowledgeable of the teachings of the New Testament, and confessing that my Jewish spirit has been enriched by them.

How, I ask myself, could I of all people be speaking to you here today of a book that until my university years I never dared to read, lest its false teachings contaminate my soul nurtured on the purity of God's authentic revelations? I was born and raised in an ultra-Orthodox home. I learned to read Hebrew before English and the Torah before "Little Red Riding Hood." I went to *cheder*, the Hebrew school, several hours each day; began the study of the Talmud before I was bar mitzvah; was trained to read from the scroll of the Torah on the Sabbath and festivals; trekked miles to attend daily morning services in the synagogue, and only when the services were over did I board the streetcar to a distant high school; and gained for myself a reputation for righteousness and piety that filled the hearts of my parents with pride and my fantasies with messianic ambition. If ever there was a life predestined for the glory of God, seemingly it was mine. I had been singled out, so it seemed to me, by God the Father to tend his vineyard and keep it free of alien and blighting growths.

But as it turned out, neither I, nor my parents, nor my teachers had read the signs aright. To be sure, I was pious, and I was Law-abiding, and I was confident that my piety and righteousness would assure for me eternal life and resurrection. Yet when I was feeling most pleased with myself and most confident of my salvation, I had a terrifying experience on the road to the synagogue. I was sixteen years old at the time and at the height of my piety and righteousness and confidence. I was more and more visualizing myself as the intrepid champion of the Law and defender of the Faith. With these goals in the forefront of my mind, I had been reading R. Traver Herford's highly appealing and sympathetic reappraisal of the Pharisees and was deeply impressed with his efforts to convey to Christian readers the inner joy that a believing Jew feels when he is yoked to the Law. Herford also exposed me to Paul for the first time, and I was appalled that anyone who had been so loyal a son of the Law could have been so out of his mind that he could have thrown over the Law for a false messiah, Jesus.

I could not help but feel a glow of pride and satisfaction that, unlike Paul, my faith and loyalty were sturdy and impregnable. Exultant, I trudged off to the synagogue for study and for the afternoon and evening prayers that would follow. It was the Sabbath, around four o'clock in the afternoon, and a baseball game was in progress on the sandlot diamond that I had to pass en route. The day was sunny and pleasant and as I paused to watch the game for a moment or two, I was flooded with pre-bar mitzvah memories of joys and ambitions that had had nothing to do with the Law. Indeed, the Law had been in the way, for it forbade playing of ball on the Sabbath, the very day that for a young boy should have been set aside for sporting events. This, it seemed to me, was asking too much. The Law may have been given by God, and it may have prohibited the playing of ball on the Sabbath, yet God's command "Thou shalt not play ball" was countermanded by an even more powerful command deep within me that proclaimed, "Thou shalt play ball, even on the Sabbath." And play ball I did, even though this meant sneaking off to some neighborhood far from my father's prying eyes.

Suddenly I was jolted out of my reverie by a terrifying thought: "What if Paul was right?" "What if the Law was not binding?" "What if behind the Law sin lurked, ready to provoke some untamed impulse to defy the Law and the God who had revealed it?" I broke out in a cold sweat and began to run, not walk, toward the synagogue. But I had great difficulty. The thought would not go away. I became more and more terrified. I was on the edge of paralysis when, by a sheer exertion of will, I marshaled my religious defenses, calmed down, and made my way to the synagogue, where my spirits and confidence were revived. Buoyed by the return of my senses, I "forgot" the tremendum that I had experienced and resumed my Lawful ways.

Though I "forgot" what had occurred, the episode itself was a portent far more prophetic than the resumption of my pious and righteous life under the Law. For it was to be only a few years later that I was to diverge from the road I had been following. At Johns Hopkins, I studied under brilliant scholars who compelled me to rethink and reevaluate all that I had taken for granted, and I was persuaded that the key to understanding both Judaism and Christianity was to be found in a critical rethinking and restructuring of the history and religion of the people of Israel. And it was in the process of carrying through this task that the New Testament was transformed for me from a book of revulsion into a book of revelation. For what I was more and more forced to acknowledge was the fact that the New Testament records not so much an irreparable break from Judaism as a mutation of Judaism, a mutation that was not recognized as such at the time because Judaism had never been thought of as a developmental religion, or Israel as a developmental people, or God as a Being so infinite and beyond human understanding that his fullness needed more than one revelation for its disclosure.

Ironically, the more I drifted away from the Law and the more I shed the unquestioning faith of my early life in Judaism, the more I was able to deepen my faith by discovering that God had given multiple revelations to Israel. The Orthodox Judaism on which I had been nurtured was not the pristine form of Judaism but rather a form of Judaism that had not been known to Moses, or Isaiah, or Ezekiel. It was not the religion of Israel as set forth in the Pentateuch. Rather, it was a mutational form of Judaism. Far from having been given on Sinai, the Oral Law had been born in the crucible of the Hasmonean revolt against Antiochus and his Jewish supporters. The belief in eternal life and resurrection that went hand in hand with the Oral Law had not been spelled out in the Pentateuch. The Scribes-Pharisees who had legitimatized this mutation had themselves exercised an authority that had no Pentateuchal warrant. The proof-texting manner in which Scriptures was now read by the Scribes-Pharisees was at odds with the way Scriptures had previously been read. The institutions that were to become bywords, the *Bet Din Hagadol* and the synagogue, were nowhere provided for in the Pentateuch. The daily reciting of the *Shema* and mandatory prayers was not called for by Pentateuchal Law. The Sadducees who insisted, with justice, that God had given only the Written Law and that the rewards and punishments spelled out by the Written Law were to be exclusively this-worldly rewards and punishments—these Sadducees were denounced by the Scribes-Pharisees and condemned to eternal damnation. Far from being the only revelation, the twofold Law of my early life in Judaism was a mutational form of Judaism that had displaced the Judaism that for several centuries had been grounded in a literal reading of the Pentateuch.

Further study revealed further complications. The Pentateuchal form of Judaism itself had been preceded by a form that had been radically different. It was a form whose hallmark was prophecy. God talked to prophets and revealed his will to them. They, the prophets, were the ultimate authorities and not the priests. Pentateuchal Judaism thus showed itself to have been a mutational form of Judaism. Its triumph had sealed the lips of the prophets by limiting God's revelation to the immutable laws given to Moses on Sinai and written down once and for all.

It thus became evident to me that the development of the religion of Israel was no simple replicating process but had been punctuated by the bursting out of unanticipated mutations. The prophets had never anticipated a day when prophecy would end. The Aaronide priesthood had never anticipated a day when the Scribes-Pharisees would sit in Moses' seat and God's revelation on

Sinai would have been of a twofold Law, Written and Oral, and not the Written Law alone. Yet the unanticipated not only occurred but became normative forms of Judaism. If normative, then God must have had the power to reveal again and again. Otherwise how could the Written Law displace prophecy and the Oral Law gain ascendency over the Written?

And to compound the complexity, I discovered that there had arisen in Alexandria a Hellenistic form of Judaism that was mutational in its own right. It was mutational because it dissolved the highly personal anthropomorphic God of the Pentateuch into the God of the philosophers and the simple stories of Genesis and Exodus into sophisticated allegories. Yet it was this transmuted Judasm that was the Judaism of Philo even though it had not been the Judaism of the prophets, or of the literal Pentateuch, or of the twofold Law of the Scribes-Pharisees.

With these three mutations spread before me, I concluded that each of these mutations must have been a bona fide revelation for those Jews who altered their beliefs and restructured their mode of life. For otherwise, that form of Judaism, that to this day is regarded as normative by most Jews, namely rabbinic Judaism, would have had no historical legitimacy.

If then I acknowledged that mutations had occurred in Judaism before the rise of Christianity and that these mutations had come to be regarded as revelations by large numbers of Jews, then I was bound to read the New Testament with an eye to the possibility that the Gospels, Acts, the Letters of Paul, and the other books of the New Testament were recording the breakout of a fourth mutation, a mutation that had been no less a revelation than the three mutations that had preceded it.

It is with this possibility in mind that I invite you to take a look with me at the New Testament. What is so striking at first glance is that we find ourselves, despite the Greek, within the framework of Judaism. The Synoptic Gospels are cast in literary forms evocative of the historical books of the Bible; the proof-texting that abounds is none other than the proof-texting we find in the Mishnah; the controversies between Jesus and the Scribes-Pharisees have no referent outside the community of Israel; Jesus' preachments of the coming of the kingdom could have had meaning only for Jews; the synagogues in which Jesus reads from the Prophets, heals the sick, and forgives sins is a Jewish house of worship for believing Jews and not unconverted Gentiles; terms such as Son of man, Messiah, and David's scion were emotion-laden for the descendants of Abraham, Isaac, and Jacob but for no others; and Jesus' last words on the cross are from a psalm and not from some alien litany.

The Book of Acts is no less Jewish than are the Synoptics. An outsider would be at a loss to find his way in this Jewish world until he had become an insider. One has only to recall the tussle that broke out between the Pharisees and the Sadducees when Paul cried out that he was being harried because of his teaching of the resurrection to appreciate how bewildering these doctrinal differences were bound to be to unbriefed Gentiles.

Even the Gospel of John does not extricate itself from the matrix of Judaism. The Gospel is addressed to Gentiles; it is rejective of the Jews as the people of God; it mounts a harsh and bitter polemic against the entire Jewish people for having crucified the Christ. Yet it is a gospel that underscores the fact that the people of Israel were the people of Christ in the flesh; it was the people to whom God the Father had sent the light; it was the people who, by failing to see the light while Christ was among them and failing to see the Christ when he was crucified, had lost their right to be the people of God to those Gentiles who had seen the light through the resurrection. But the postresurrection people of God are not cut off from the Israel to whom Christ had been sent in the flesh. Far from it. The Gospel of John, like the Synoptic Gospels, feels compelled to proof-text John's claims from Scripture with the implication that if scriptural proof were lacking, his claims that the Christians were the true people of God would be worthless. The fact that in his time Israel consisted overwhelmingly of Gentiles was beside the point if it were indeed true that the God of Israel had sent his son to his people in the flesh and they had rejected him. There was, after all, good biblical and Pharisaic precedent for God's casting off those of his people Israel, like the Sadducees, who had violated the covenant and, though born to Israel of the flesh, were cast out of Israel of the spirit.

Now it is true, of course, that the Gospel of John raises some very sticky questions, not so much in principle as in practice. In the past, however large the number of Jews who had been deemed outcasts and however large the number of Gentiles who had converted to Judaism, the majority of the Jewish people consisted of Jews who had been born into the faith and nurtured on it. Not so, however, with the Christian community that the Gospel of John bespeaks. This community consisted predominately of Gentiles who laid claim to being the true Israel because they had come to believe in the risen Christ while the Jews had not. Though in principle this should have made no difference, in fact it made a great deal of difference because it meant that the constituents of this new Israel had had no experience of having belonged to the Israel that was being displaced. All that they knew was that Jesus had been rejected by his people and had been accepted by them. The Jesus of the Synoptics who had come to bring the good news of the coming of the kingdom of God to his people; the Jesus who fits so tightly into the contours of real time and real space; one who heals the sick, exorcises the demon-haunted, and comforts the poor; a charismatic of flesh and blood even though he was to become more than he seemed to have been—this Jesus is dissolved in the Gospel of John into the Divine Light that should have been seen by the Jews but was not. It was the Jesus who had lived so that he might die and reveal the divine self that he had always been through the medium of the resurrection. And since the Jews had failed to recognize the Divine Light while Jesus had been alive and had failed to recognize the Divine Light when he had been resurrected, what need was there for believing Gentiles to have any knowledge of the historical Jewish Jesus at all? A Christian community could thus lay claim to being the true Israel; could call upon Scriptures to justify these claims; and yet could have no knowledge of what it was to have been born and raised as a Jew.

A community such as John's, which needed nothing but the resurrection, was an anomaly indeed. But its anomalous status does not extricate it from its rootage. It does not cease to be a mutation of Israel simply because it is a community consisting almost exclusively of Gentiles. This, I think, will become evident when we turn to Paul.

With Paul, we are on more secure ground. By his own testimony, he had been born a Jew, and a precocious one at that. He had been as to the Law a Pharisee and as to righteousness under the Law blameless. Indeed he had prided himself on having been more advanced in Judaism than others his own age, so zealous had he been for the Traditions of the Fathers. This precociousness and zeal had gone hand in hand with Paul's violent persecution of the church.

How, then, did Paul, the zealous champion of the twofold Law, come to Christ? He came to Christ because he saw Jesus Christ risen from the dead, not because he wanted to see him risen but because he could not help seeing him resurrected and alive. What Paul had thought was a blasphemous claim had been transformed for him into an undeniable fact. He had been wrong, grievously so. Having witnessed with his own eyes the risen Christ, Paul had to bring his conception of Judaism into line with this astonishing fact.

Paul's conception of Judaism had been the conception that had been taught by the Scribes-Pharisees. It was the Judaism of the twofold Law and it was the Judaism that preached eternal life for the soul and the resurrection of the body. It was a form of Judaism that rejected the Judaism of the Sadducees as spurious and heretical, and it was a form of Judaism that was incongruent with the Hellenistic form of Judaism flourishing in Philo's Alexandria. It was a form of Judaism whose leaders were teachers and not prophets. It was, in fact, a form of Judaism that was mutational, even though for Paul and the Scribes-Pharisees it was believed to have been designed at Sinai. When, therefore, Paul was zealously persecuting the followers of Jesus for claiming that Jesus had risen from the dead and was the Christ, he was persecuting them not as a Sadducee or as a Philonic philosopher or as a prophet but as a follower of the Pharisees and as a preacher of the good news of eternal life and resurrection, beliefs that were in Paul's day still being denounced as heretical by the Sadducees. As a teacher of the twofold Law and as a preacher of eternal life and resurrection, Paul was absolutely convinced that the resurrection of the dead was not only possible but inevitable for those who adhered to the twofold Law and who listened to the teachings of the Scribes-Pharisees. For Paul, then, the issue had never been whether Jesus could have been resurrected, as it would have been for a Sadducee, but whether he had been resurrected. When, therefore, Paul persecuted those who were preaching the risen Christ, he was not persecuting them because they believed that there would be a resurrection but because they claimed that Jesus had been resurrected and that this resurrection was proof positive that Jesus must be the Christ.

For Paul, this was an impossibility since Jesus had during his lifetime challenged the Scribes-Pharisees and had refused to knuckle under to their authority. How, then, could Jesus have been resurrected when a precondition for resurrection was the acknowledgment of the authority of the Scribes-Pharisees to determine what was right law and what was right doctrine? Since the answer to this question was that Jesus could not have been resurrected, Paul acted accordingly and sought to root out the preachers of this blasphemous heresy. But when he himself saw the risen Christ, he was forced to face the implications of this fact—and face it he did.

Since, Paul reasoned, Jesus had risen from the dead even though Jesus had challenged the Scribes-Pharisees during his lifetime, the teachings of the Pharisees must be seriously flawed. Adherence to the twofold Law could not in and of itself guarantee eternal life and resurrection since Jesus had risen from the dead even though he had defied the authoritative teachers of the twofold Law. The road to resurrection, therefore, could not be the road of the Law but a road marked out by the resurrection of Jesus and its meaning.

For Paul, this meaning was to be found in a weakness inherent not in the Law itself but in the human condition. The Law is indeed divine and good, but the individual is a slave of sin. The Law may temporarily damn up the impulse to sin, but sooner or later sin will have its way. Indeed, the Law lends itself to manipulation by sin since the "Thou shalt nots" of the Law only goad our sinful impulses to respond defiantly with "Thou shalt." The Law thus serves as an agent provocateur of sin. To look to the Law for salvation is to be put off guard since it diverts us from focusing on sin and its power and on our human condition and its helplessness.

This, then, must be the meaning of the resurrection. God, knowing of man's helplessness in the face of sin, sent Jesus Christ so that, through his death and through his resurrection, man might dissolve his sinful impulses in response to Christ's unconditional love. Whereas the Law provokes sin, Christ's love dissolves it.

It is here in Paul's radical critique of the Law that Jews and

Christians have tended to see the parting of the ways. And with good reason. For if the Law is the essence of Judaism, then it would follow that Paul's rejection of the Law would ipso facto be a rejection of Judaism.

But is the Law the essence of Judaism? This is the root question to which we must now seek an answer.

At first glance, the answer would seem to be obvious enough. Paul stresses in both Philippians and Galatians his precocious relationship to the Law. In Romans, chapter 7, he clearly identifies the Law as having been essential to Judaism prior to the resurrection of Jesus. But a more penetrating analysis does not yield so clear-cut a conclusion. For though it is indeed true that for the Scribes-Pharisees adherence to the twofold Law was essential for salvation and for the Sadducees adherence to the literal commands of the Pentateuch was a sine qua non, it had not been all true for such prophets as Amos, Hosea, Micah, and Isaiah. These prophets regarded righteousness, justice, and loving-kindness as the essence of God's covenant with Israel and not the Law. Not a single one of these prophets even mentions Sinai. Not a single one of these prophets recalls Moses as a lawgiver. Not a single one of these prophets regarded sacrifices as mandatory: "I hate your Sabbaths, I despise your feasts, and I reject your sacrifices, but let justice roll down like water and righteousness like an everlasting stream" is the leitmotiv first enunciated by Amos. For prophets such as these, the Sabbath, the festivals, and the cultus were allowable so long as they did not deflect the people from what was essential to the covenant—namely God's singularity, God's attributes (justice, mercy, and loving-kindness), and Israel's commitment to this God and to his attributes.

The teachings of these grand prophets thus preclude the Law as being essential to the covenant, however important the Law became for subsequent forms of Judaism. But is this not also evident from the fact that the Written Law, the Pentateuch, is a radically different Law from the twofold Law proclaimed by the Scribes-Pharisees? One has only to flip through the titles of the tractates of the Mishnah to become aware that this repository of the Oral Law deals with categories of Law, such as *Berachot* (Blessings); *Ketubot* (Marriage Contracts); *Yadayim* (Uncleanness of Hands); *Eruvin* (Sabbath Limits), that are not even mentioned in the Pentateuch.

After all, there would have been no point for Paul to have prided himself on having been "as to the Law a Pharisee" if there was only one Law to which all Jews adhered. Thus not only do the prophets such as Amos testify to the fact that the essence of the covenant was not Law, but the fact that there could be such a cleavage as to what the Law was—a cleavage that during the reign of Alexander Janneus pitted the Pharisees and Sadducees against each other in a savage civil war—clearly reveals that the Law was a superimposition, not an essence. Both before the Law and beyond the Law, the essence of Judaism continued to be as it was for the prophets: God's singularity and his attributes of justice, mercy, and loving-kindness.

But it is not only retrospectively that we discern a form of Judaism, namely the prophetic, that did not acknowledge the Law as the essence of the religion of Israel, but we discern it also in the existence of a form of Judaism in our own day that likewise does not regard the Law as the essence of Judaism. This form of Judaism is flourishing, and its seminary, the Hebrew Union College-Jewish Institute of Religion, trains rabbis for Reform congregations both in the United States and abroad. There can be no question that this seminary is a seminary devoted to the teaching and the perpetuation of Judaism. It may be denounced as a seedbed of heresy by the ultra-Orthodox, it may even be viewed by them as worse than a Christian seminary, but it is regarded by friend and foe alike as a Jewish institution. Yet Reform Judaism does not recognize the binding character of either the Written or Oral Law nor the Orthodox claims that God had revealed his total revelation to Moses on Sinai. Instead, Reform Judaism affirms that God's revelation is ongoing and that the essence of Judaism is to be found in the singularity of God and in his attributes of justice, mercy, and loving-kindness.

Reform Judaism thus bears witness to the fact that Pharisaism was not the last mutation-revelation in Judaism for Reform Judaism is as legitimate a mutation-revelation for Jews who acknowledge it as such as were the Pentateuchal and Pharisaic mutations-revelations for those Jews who adopted these mutations-revelations as normative. If, then, Reform Judaism can be Judaism without the Law, the Law cannot be the essence of Judaism for those who have adopted Reform Judaism as normative. And if there can be a Judaism unrooted in the Law in our own day, by what right can I as a Reform Jew read Paul out of Judaism merely because in his day Jews believed that the Law was the essence of Judaism? So long as Paul insisted, as he did, that the Christ was sent by the one God of Israel to redeem humankind from the bondage of sin, and so long as he justified his revelation of Christ by an appeal to Scriptures, and so long as he proclaimed that the followers of Christ were the Israel of the spirit, I see no way of denying to Paul's teachings the right to be categorized as a mutation-revelation of Judaism for all those Jews or Gentiles who accept these teachings as normative without at the same time denying not only the right of Reform Judaism to be categorized as a mutation-revelation but of Orthodox Judaism as well—a form of Judaism that owes its own legitimacy to a mutation-revelation. And as for Gentiles, there is in principle no way to exclude the possibility that a community of Israel could emerge consisting of a majority who were either converts themselves or the children of converts unless there is some quota or cutoff point for new converts. In principle, even the most extreme Orthodox rabbi cannot countenance such a quota or cutoff so long as the convert fulfills all the legal requirements. The fact then that Pauline Christianity spread almost exclusively among Gentiles does not in and of itself derogate from Pauline Christianity's right to be regarded as a mutation-revelation within Judaism, so long as the community affirms that it is the Israel of the spirit. Hence when we read the Gospel of John and recognize that it is a gospel that is speaking to a Christian community consisting of Gentiles, we are confronted by an anomaly, but not by a new religion. John may be addressing Gentiles and he may be rejecting Jews, but he is not rejecting either the God of Israel or the authority of Scriptures. He is affirming that Jesus was a Jew in the flesh, that he was sent by God, the Father, to the Jews, who failed to recognize him, and became the Christ for all those who did so recognize him either during his earthly sojourn or after his resurrection. The Jews were not cut off from Christ; they cut themselves off. Christ did not come for the Gentiles but for all humankind. The fact that Gentiles and not Jews acknowledged him as the Christ was simply a fact, not a destiny.

If then I read the New Testament as the record of a mutation-revelation within the framework of Judaism, what do I do with the hostility that suffuses the Gospels and the Epistles of Paul? What do I do with Matthew 23 and its condemnation of the Scribes-Pharisees as whitewashed tombs, venemous vipers, and sons of hell? How do I react to the trial and crucifixion of Jesus and the harsh judgment leveled against the Jews for their complicity?

I answer these questions by facing them head-on. What, after all, is one to expect? Sweetness and light, genteel polemic, serene travail when a charismatic of charismatics challenges the authority of the Scribes-Pharisees, exposes the Jews to Roman wrath by preaching the coming of God's kingdom and not the continuity of Caesar's kingdom, attracts crowds who could go berserk, causes a rumpus in the Temple area in the midst of maddening crowds, evokes shouts of "Long live the King of the Jews," "Long live the son of David, Hosanna in the highest" and neither affirms or denies that he is the King of the Jews?

Those were harsh and unruly times. Judea had proved to be ungovernable. There was not a day without its violence, a week without its demonstrations, a year without its insurrections. The Roman emperors did not know how to keep the peace; the procurators did not know how to keep the peace; the high priest and his privy council did not know how to keep the peace. Repression did not work, permissiveness did not work, muddle did not work. When John the Baptist preached repentance and baptism, he was put to death not because of his teachings but because he attracted crowds, and crowds were unpredictable and dangerous. Even those religious leaders who, as in the case of John, may have been sympathetic to his religious revivalism were frightened lest a naive charismatic unintentionally spark an insurrection that would lead to devastating reprisals on the entire people. Hence it is not surprising that everyone did what he did because nobody knew what else to do.

In this maelstrom of violence and anarchy, no charismatic was likely to come out alive, least of all a gentle charismatic with no political ambitions, only a prophetic impulse to awaken his people to the coming of God's kingdom. To the degree that his teachings found a hearing and to the degree that his preachings attracted crowds of listeners and to the degree that his wonder-working aroused awe, to that degree was he bound to attract the attention of the high priest, appointed by the procurator, and arouse his concern. All that was needed was some incident that spelled potential danger and his fate was sealed.

For Jesus' disciples this fate was intolerable. Here was their gentle Teacher being arrested by the orders of the high priest, tried by the high priest's council, and crucified by Pontius Pilate acting on the judgment of the high priest and his council, and they, his disciples, were to be unmoved? Seeing their Teacher brutally crucified, were they to remain unbitter? Or were they to cry out in their pain and anguish and lash out at all those who had been in any way party to this gruesome deed?

And was not their bitterness compounded when bruised, stunned, and bewildered by the seeming death of their beloved Teacher, they saw Jesus risen from the dead, proclaimed the good news, and found themselves rebuked and hounded from the synagogue by the very Scribes-Pharisees who had taught them to believe in the resurrection of the dead? How, then, can I be surprised if I find the Gospels full of bitterness, recrimination, and anathemas? After all, if Jesus' disciples were human beings of flesh and blood, am I to expect them to respond to pain, anguish, and harassment with divine transcendence? I would expect them to be angry, bitter, and vengeful, as indeed the Gospels portray them as having been.

But their bitterness, their anger, and vengefulness has nothing to do with anti-Semitism. Rather it was the normal by-product of mutations-revelations in Judaism, and in Christianity as well. We have evidence enough of this in the struggle between the Pharisees and the Sadducees. Not only did the Pharisees and Sadducees denounce each other as heretics, but they slugged it out in a bloody, generation-long civil war. And when the Pharisees regained power, they wreaked vengeance on Diogenes and others who had counseled Alexander Janneus to crucify 800 followers of the Pharisees.

In subsequent epochs, Rabbanites and Karaites, Maimonists and anti-Maimonists, Chasidim and Mitnagdim hurled vituperation at one another, read one another out of the faith, and would have translated their harsh words into violent deeds if this option had been open to them.

And when we turn to the history of Christianity, is it not marked by violent confrontations between the followers of Christ? Is there any diatribe in the New Testament against the Scribes-Pharisees that has not been outdone by Luther? Is there any act of harassment by the Scribes-Pharisees against the followers of Jesus more harassing than the decades of religious wars that followed the Protestant Reformation? Yet such intense collisions are looked upon as intra-Christian struggles and not as interreligious struggles. So why should we not look upon the collisions recorded in the New Testament as intra-Jewish collisions and not the collision of two separate religions?

When, therefore, I look at the New Testament, I see a precious record of the birth of Judaism's fourth mutation-revelation, with all the travail that attends such a birth. And like the mutations-revelations that preceded it and the mutations-revelations that followed it, the New Testament seems to me to display two levels, divine light and the human prism. For like all previous revelations, I see this revelation, too, as being refracted through human prisms. As a consequence, the divine light is not simply reflected but is fractured. What I find in the New Testament is a commingling of light and shadow; and it is this commingling that explains for me the ease with which anti-Semites have exploited the bitter, harsh, and vengeful sayings in the New Testament to justify the harassment and the persecution of the Jews through the centuries. Focusing on the Gospel accounts of the trial and crucifixion of Jesus, anti-Semites have been able to whip up the passions of the mob by accusing the Jews of being Christ killers, host desecraters, ritual murderers, well poisoners, and children of Satan. Confronted by such animus and hostility proof-texted from the New Testament, Jews couldn't possibly see any divine light emanating from a Christ imprisoned within texts bursting with hostility and vengefulness. Little wonder then that when I was growing up, Christ was an anathema and not a redeemer, the New Testament a blasphemy and not a revelation.

Despite these barriers, however, I found it possible through a deeper understanding of how God reveals himself to Israel through mutations-revelations, each one of which showing itself to have been a commingling of divine light and human shadow, to vault over barriers and find, snuggling behind the hostility and vengefulness, a Christ of compassion, graciousness, and love. This Christ bore no resemblance to the Christ of hatred and vengeance. It was a Christ who forgave the Jews because they did not know what they were doing. It was this Christ that in some way may have been reaching out to me when, puffed with pride and righteousness, I was terrified by the unwilled thought "What if Paul was right?" and was confronted with the haunting possibility that deep within me was an impulse to defy the Law that might prove to be more powerful than the impulse to obey it.

But I did not become a Christian even when I did part from the Law and even when I concluded that the New Testament was a mutation-revelation within Judaism and that Paul's radical critique of the Law and his proclamation that the true Israel was the Israel of the spirit and not of the flesh were as legitimate an expression of Judaism's quest for the fullness of God as the Pharisaic proclamation that God had given two Laws, not one. I did not become a Christian because to have done so would have deprived me of the revelations that had preceded the rise of Christianity and the revelations that were to follow. I would have cut myself off from a divine odyssey that reaches back to the Patriarchs and reaches forward to the Messianic Age, an odyssey of a people ever searching for the fullness of God. It is a odyssey that a people of flesh and spirit undergoes, and it is this odyssey that is for Jews, such as myself, the ultimate revelation. For what we find spread before us is a record of continuous revelation to and through the Jews—revelations through prophets, through books, through Scribes-Pharisees, through philosophers, through Christ-Jesus, through rationalists, through Kabbalists, through charismatics, through Reformers, and even through Jewish secularists and nationalists.

And all to what end? To make manifest through the history of a people God's faith in humankind's capacity for shaping a world that God can pronounce as good, very good indeed. For if we open our Bibles to the first verses of Genesis, we read that God created heaven and earth and all that is therein and that he capped his creation with a single individual, formed in his image and after his likeness, an individual whom God entrusted with his goodly creation. God looked upon the whole world he had created as goodly and not just some special land, territory, or place. God had also created a single individual, male and female, and not a multitude of people. And this individual was not an Egyptian, or a Babylonian, or a Frenchman, or an American, or a Jew. He was just an individual, as God was an individual, but what an individual, created as he was in the image of God! God's commitment was thus not to a race or nation or class or mob but to the individual.

And God put this individual into a paradise that the individual had not earned but that would provide him with every good, without effort, provided that he forswore knowledge and responsibility for making religious, moral, and ethical choices.

This the individual was unable to do. Therefore, God cast him out of paradise and plunged him into history, where he might strive to regain paradise by refining his religious, moral, and ethical choices.

But when it became evident that human beings were not at all choosing wisely, God, in a decision of last resort, decided to experiment with a single people and chose Abraham to father a nation that would keep alive the belief in the one God who had created a goodly universe, who had capped his creation with an individual in his own image and after his own likeness, and who had given this individual and his descendants the power to discriminate between good and evil.

This people, which Abraham fathered, was thus launched by God on an odyssey that could not come to an end until humankind had so refined its religious sensitivities that it would freely choose good over evil and regain for itself a paradise that this time it had earned through pain, suffering, anguish, and knowledge. Throughout the centuries this people of God clung to their faith and they clung to their hopes, however tempestuous the waters and however crushing the breakers. This they were able to do because they were continuously being buoyed up by revelations that assured them that God still cared and that God would not totally abandon them, even when they seemed to be abandoning him.

Among the revelations along the way was the revelation that has come down to us in the New Testament. It was a divine revelation, a revelation that vividly personified God's loving compassion for every individual, but it was a revelation that, because few Jews were able to see it as such, found its home among the Gentiles. For the first time in all of Israel's history, a revelation of God to his people had brought life and light to Gentiles who had known him not but who knew him now—and another people of God was launched on its odyssey with its own unique and special destiny.

But the Jews persisted in their own uniqueness and continued to spawn revelations, revelations that sustained their faith and their hope even when, as a tiny minority among Christians and Muslims (who, in affirming Islam, were in their own unique way bearing witness to still another mutation), they were continuously being mocked for their stubbornness and persecuted for their stiff-neckness. They gave the lie, however, to their detractors by continuing to bear spiritual fruit: two Talmuds, Midrash, commentaries without end, ethical treatises, mystical probings, philosophic forays, liturgical gems, and poetic flights.

The Jewish people were sustained by revelations in the modern age as well, as gifted religious leaders, teachers, and philosophers searched for more of God and found it. They did not fall prey to secularism, nor were they stripped of their religious questing by the triumphs of Jewish nationalism—a nationalism whose own claims to nationhood are gleaned from God-saturated Scriptures and whose enduring national heritage from the past are spiritual and not political triumphs. So sturdy indeed is this people of God that not even the Holocaust could extinguish its spirit.

The Jewish people is thus very much alive today for, it seems to me, their divine odyssey is not yet at an end. Humankind has still not recognized that God is One, that his universe is a goodly one, and that every individual is created in his image and after his likeness. The end of days, which the prophets preached, is still far off. The meaning of the Jewish odyssey has yet to be assimilated. Paradise has not yet been regained. A re-genesis still eludes us. The need of Israel for multiple revelations is still manifest to those Jews, like myself, who see and feel this need.

This, then, explains how I, a Jew, can look at the New Testament and read it as a record of a revelation-mutation and yet not become a Christian. For whereas a true Christian is totally fulfilled in Christ and needs no other revelation, I cannot be so fulfilled. I cannot be so fulfilled because I have become convinced that so long as God reveals himself through human instruments, every revelation is partial. I therefore feel the need for all the revelations that were given to Israel in the past, all the revelations that are being given to Israel in the present, and all the revelations that may be given to Israel in the future until the ushering in of the Messianic Age gives us, at long last, the fullness of God.

Convinced that until that end of days the divine light will always be refracted through human prisms and convinced at the same time that the divine light will always be straining to break through, I do not wish to have the light streaming toward me and yet see it not.

VI
THE MEANING OF MESSIAH IN JEWISH THOUGHT

A paper delivered at the Southern Baptist-Jewish Scholars Conference sponsored by the Home Mission Board of the Southern Baptist Convention and the Department of Interreligious Affairs of the American Jewish Committee at the Southern Baptist Theological Seminary (Louisville, KY), 18–20 August 1969.

Published in *Union Seminary Quarterly Review*, vol. XXVI, no. 4 (Summer 1971), pp. 383–406.

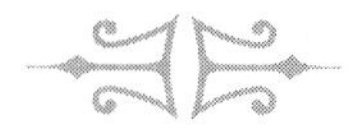

In addressing myself to the problem of the meaning of Messiah in Jewish thought, I come as a historian seeking to make the past intelligible. I am interested in trying to comprehend how an idea comes into existence, how it develops, how it spreads, and how it diverges into different highways and byways. Since, however, the problem is so complex and the theme so rich and the space so short, I shall concentrate primarily on the process of gestation.

Let me begin with some facts that are relatively secure. First, Christianity does not antedate the ministry of Jesus. Second, the New Testament quotes freely from the Old Testament to underwrite the claim that Jesus is the Christ. Third, the history of Jews and Judaism had been long and complex prior to the ministry of Jesus. Fourth, to render Jesus and his claims intelligible, we must know what Judaism was in his day, what it had previously been, and how the Old Testament had come to be used as a divine source for contemporary problems. Fifth, *prior* to the time of Jesus, no messianic claim had survived the death of the would-be messiah. Sixth, the belief that Jesus was the resurrected Christ has proved to be one of the most powerful beliefs in the history of mankind. Seventh, most Jews rejected Jesus as the Christ at the time and most Jews reject him now. Eighth, Jews harbored a belief that the Messiah would come but shied away from recognizing any claimant.

The historian must therefore concern himself with the following questions: (1) Why did the notion of the Messiah gain credence around the time of Jesus and not earlier? (2) Why did the claims of Jesus have so unique an impact? (3) Why did the spokesmen for Judaism on the one hand reject Jesus as the messiah while on the other they did begin to take the concept of the Messiah seriously? (4) Why did Judaism foster the belief in the Messiah throughout the Middle Ages and into modern times and yet persistently reject every claimant?

For these questions, I propose a simple answer: The emergence of the messianic idea as a viable concept in the time of Jesus, its powerful embodiment in the proclamation of Jesus as the resurrected Christ, and its ambivalent status within Judaism stem from the interaction of three factors: (1) the prevailing system of authority; (2) the challenge of changing historical conditions; (3) the range of problem-solving options.

The emergence of the messianic idea as viable and vital was not evolutionary and developmental. It was mutational. It did not follow as an immanent necessity from biblical Judaism. It was not spawned directly by the visions of Israel's prophets. It emerged spontaneously as a solution to a series of problems that Judaism had to face in the Greco-Roman world, problems for which there were no direct solutions in the Pentateuch.

Prophetic and Priestly Authority

During the biblical period—more than a thousand years—problems confronting Israel had been solved by Yahweh. At any given time during the biblical period, Israel knew where it stood not by reading a text but by consulting the prophet. When, for example, Jeremiah proclaimed that Yahweh would destroy Yahweh's house, he was speaking in Yahweh's name. When Ezekiel visualized the reconstituted Temple and the restructured Israel, he gave Yahweh as his source, not proof-texts. When Isaiah depicted the Suffering Servant and his fate, he did not appeal to a verse in Amos or Hosea. He simply affirmed, "Thus saith Yahweh."

Yahweh was thus Israel's problem solver. A tiny people, itself divided, settled within a slip of land between gigantic empires, had only Yahweh to save them. Their prophets, certain of Yahweh's omnipotence and steadfast in their faith in his promise, clutched at this solution and that. They had to determine, in the face of bewildering circumstances, Yahweh's will with respect to monarchy in general and to the Davidic line in particular. They had to wrestle not only with the problem of who should serve as priests but whether there should be priests at all. They had to make the awesome decision as to what Yahweh's covenant demanded. They had to determine whether Yahweh would countenance the destruction of Land and Temple and send his people into exile. For these questions—and a host of others—there were no clear-cut, unambiguous, immutable answers in a sacred text. Yahweh's authority had to be invoked to solve each specific problem as it arose. Hence no past prophet could bind a future one.

During the Exile and the Restoration, the problems became especially complex. Ideal expectations had to be balanced by realistic possibilities. Such questions as the following had to be answered: Was Yahweh *committed* to the restoration of the Davidic monarchy? Was Yahweh *committed* to an elaborate cultus and a hierocracy? Was Yahweh *committed* even to the prophets forever? The answers, as we know from Ezekiel, the Second Isaiah, Haggai, Zechariah, Malachi, Nehemiah, and Ezra, were both yes and no.

Yet a definitive answer was ultimately given when the canonized Pentateuch became operative in the restored Judea. Prophecy was extinguished, monarchical claims brushed aside, and Aaronide hegemony confirmed. When once and for all God's revelation to Moses was elevated above all other revelations and when Yahweh's command that the sons of Aaron enjoy an eternal monopoly over the expiatory cultic system was implemented, there was no longer any role for the prophet to play. Since he could not challenge Mosaic legislation proclaimed by Yahweh to be binding on *all* generations, his access to Yahweh's will was blocked. Similarly, so long as the Aaronide priests exercised absolute authority over the restored people by virtue of Mosaic fiat and Persian imperial decree, a king would be a problem, not a solution.

The canonization of the Pentateuch and the triumph of Aaronide absolutism thus relegated prophetic activity to the period of Israel's history when the people had needed prophets because of Israel's disloyalty. Prophetic utterances, however Yahwistically inspired, were solutions to specific problems of an age gone by. Predictions of a restored Davidic monarchy were no longer taken seriously for any such restoration would have undercut Aaronide absolutism and operational Pentateuchalism. The withering away of prophecy effectively cut off any challenge to Aaronidism since a bid for monarchical restoration would have had to have had the sanction of Yahweh.

For the Aaronides, therefore, all of Holy Scripture was read in the light of Pentateuchal primacy. This meant that God had given an eternal and immutable revelation to Moses and, hence, the only real task of Israel was absolute obedience to the Mosaic Law. Israel's failure to do this in the past had necessitated prophets and kings. However, now that the community was reorganized under the Aaronides as God had originally intended, there was no need for any other authority. If problems arose, the Aaronides and not prophets would deal with them. If unanticipated situations required decisions, the Aaronides and not kings would make them. Yahweh's continuous presence was now manifest in the expiatory system, centering in the Temple and ministered by a dedicated priesthood.

Aaronide hegemony rendered prophecy obsolete because it was a system that worked. Following on the canonization of the Pentateuch (sometime no later than the beginning of the fourth century B.C.E.), the Aaronides effectively exercised sovereignty over Israel for no less than two hundred years. The only serious rift in all this time was the Samaritan schism, but this threat was averted when the dissenters hied themselves off to Samaria and built a temple for themselves. Aside then from this challenge to Aaronide supremacy, there was no other till Jason bought the high priesthood from Antiochus and had his brother Onias, the legitimate high priest, ousted.

These two centuries of almost unruffled sovereignty testify to the operational potency of Pentateuchalism and Aaronide absolutism. This record exposed the preexilic history of Israel and Judah as functionally ineffective. In contrast to the inner divisiveness of Israel's early history marked by kings, prophets, priests, and Baalists striving for supremacy and the continuous violent intrusion of powers from without, the Aaronides exercised the hegemony granted them by the Penatateuch so efficiently and in so balanced and judicious a fashion that they stirred up no potent rivals from within and provoked no serious dissatisfaction from without. So smoothly in fact did the Aaronides run things that when Alexander wrested Judea from the Persians, he confirmed the high priest's autonomy; when the Ptolemies made good their claims to Coele-Syria, they, too, were pleased to reconfirm the Aaronidic privileges; and when the Seleucids took over from the Ptolemies, their first impulse was to leave Aaronide supremacy untouched.

What need then was there for prophecy during these years? To solve nonexistent problems? What need for a voice crying in the wilderness proclaiming the name of the Lord, when the Lord's name was being proclaimed daily, weekly, monthly, and on a variety of festal occasions? Was Israel to be delivered from such steadfast loyalty to Yahweh by a king, prophet, or messianic savior? Yahweh was secure; his Law was secure; his people were secure; his priesthood was secure; his Temple was secure; the record of his providential care of Israel in the past was secure; even the oracles of his beloved prophets were secure. What need then of a vision of the end of days, of eschaton, of a dream of Israel restored to its land and to its God?

There was no need; hence, there was no vision. For more than two hundred years, no person appeared and no book was written that was concerned with the end of days. Yet there were many sensitive spirits, and many of these committed their feelings and opinions to writing. Psalms were composed; words of wisdom set down; meditations over life's vanities shared; God's inscrutable ways with man pondered; stories told; chronicles compiled. But where in the postexilic Psalms is there a longing for the end of days, a Messiah? The postexilic Psalmist addresses himself to God; he wants a relationship with him; he yearns to have a Fortress, a Refuge, a Rock for support, protection, and hope. And where in Proverbs, Ecclesiastes, or Job is there a concern for the eschaton? Is the end of days in the burden of Esther or Ruth or Tobit?

The triumph of operational Pentateuchalism thus relegated the historical and prophetic books to dormancy. Though recognized as sacred, even inspirational, they could not be drawn upon to challenge either the Pentateuch or Aaronide hegemony. To underwrite, confirm, enhance—yes; to undermine, question, dismantle—no. The appropriate stance toward the non-Pentateuchal books, to former kings, to prophets is revealed by Ben Sira in his *Ecclesiasticus*. Here one finds Aaronide hegemony both taken for granted and jubilantly reaffirmed. Even the glory of Moses pales before that of Aaron. Though Ben Sira proclaims that Moses *revealed* God's Law, the revelation is primarily concerned with the establishment of Aaron's role as the Grand Expiator, the sacred curator of the Tent of Meeting (Tabernacle), the guardian of an uncontaminated altar, an altar on which only he and his sons might burn the sacrifices to God. This hegemony, unlike that of Moses', was to be exercised exclusively and forever by Aaron's descendants (*Sirach* 45:1–24; 50: 1–21).

When, therefore, Ben Sira turns to the other worthies of ancient Israel, be they leaders like Joshua, kings like David, or prophets like Elijah (*Sirach* 46–49), he takes for granted that nothing he says about them—or that was said by them or about them—will be taken as incompatible with Pentateuchal supremacy and Aaronide absolutism. So long as the Aaronides exercised hegemony, they, and they alone, determined what sacred Scriptures meant.

Had the Aaronides successfully exercised sovereignty throughout the Greco-Roman period, the messianic seed embedded in the oracles of the prophets would never have sprouted branches or borne fruit. The two hundred years of dormancy under the Aaronides is evidence enough. But the Aaronides did not succeed in exercising their hegemony. They were toppled from power by their failure to solve the problem presented by Hellenization.

The collapse of Aaronide hegemony had followed on a crisis of confidence: Jason, a brother of the high priest Onias, bought for himself the high priesthood from Antiochus. This was a flagrant violation of Pentateuchal Law. Its flagrancy was compounded by the fact that it was an effort to foster Hellenization. When this misdeed was followed by the ousting of Jason by Meneleus, an even more radical Hellenist, the vast majority of Pentateuchally loyal Judeans suddenly found themselves bereft of leadership; at a time when their religion was faced with its most serious crisis in more than two hundred years, there was no legitimate high priest to guide them.

The Pharisaic Revolution

It was this crisis of confidence that spawned a new class of leaders. Though they are better known to us as the Pharisees, they called themselves Soferim, Scribes. However, they were not the Soferim whom Ben Sira describes. The latter had been Aaronide supremacists, intellectual devotees of literal Pentateuchalism. They had exercised no power over the Law. They had supported Aaronide supremacy and literal Pentateuchalism. Their métier had been Wisdom: the proverb, the parable, the simile, the bon mot, the riddle, the paradox. They had praised the Pentateuch, the Aaronides, Wisdom. They had *not* determined the Law; nor had they applied exegesis to it. They knew nothing of an Oral Law. For them, the *literal* Pentateuch was the Law; and the *literal* Pentateuch was more concerned with Aaronide absolutism than it was with anything else.

By contrast, the Soferim who supplanted the Aaronides claimed absolute authority over the Law. They proclaimed that God had given Moses not only the Written Law but the Oral Law as well, making the Law twofold, not one. This twofold Law, they stressed, had been transmitted from Moses to Joshua, to the elders, to the prophets, and most recently to the Soferim-Pharisees. They also claimed that the Aaronides had never been the transmitters of the Law; that they were cultic functionaries, not legal authorities. Their job was limited to the administration of the cult and the offering of sacrifices. It was evident to the Soferim that, except for Aaron and Eleazar, no Aaronide had ever been vouchsafed a direct revelation from Yahweh. In the years following the death of Moses and Joshua, God had spoken to judges and to prophets, but never to an Aaronide. A Jeremiah and Ezekiel may have been priests, but they had spoken in Yahweh's name as prophets, even when they spoke of priestly concerns.

God's teachings, so these Soferim declared, were not confined to the Pentateuch. Although not a letter was to be added to the Written Law, there was no such restriction on the Oral Law. For the Oral Law was not so much a Law of content as a principle of ongoing authority to take the Law in one's hand. The prophet had not been bound by Pentateuchal Law when threatened; the viability of the Law itself was threatened. The historical and prophetic books revealed that the prophets had again and again acted contrary to Pentateuchal Law, even though they added not so much as a word to the Pentateuch. Their authority had been ongoing. So long as they did not insert their teachings in the Pentateuch, they had had the right to determine at any given moment what the Law demanded.

Such teachings of the Soferim-Pharisees were radically new. The concept of the twofold Law had not existed earlier. The right of Soferim to exercise authority over the Law had no Pentateuchal support. Indeed, such an authority is nowhere to be found within all of Holy Writ. Even Ezra the Scribe wields authority by virtue of his pedigree linking him to Zadok, Phineas, Eleazar, and Aaron (Ezra 7:1–6) and not by virtue of Scribal authority. Nonetheless, this new class of Soferim sits itself in Moses' seat, proclaims a twofold Law without any authorization from the Pentateuch, even as it reaffirms the Pentateuch as the Word of God and Moses the prophet nonpareil.

This new class of Soferim-Pharisees were thus "revolutionaries."[1] They taught doctrines of startling novelty. They proclaimed that the God of revelation was the Heavenly Father of the individual. He was not simply the Father of the Patriarchs or the Father of Israel but the Father of each and every person. It was out of fatherly concern that he revealed to Israel the twofold Law for it was the path to individual salvation. Here he had clearly mapped out the road to eternal life and resurrection. For the *individual* who internalized the system of the twofold Law and guided his life by it, there was the promise of an eternal individuation.

[1]The revolutionary role of the Pharisees has hitherto been overlooked by both Jewish and Christian scholars. I have sought to develop the concept of the Pharisaic revolution in the following studies: "The Internal City," *Journal for the Scientific Study of Religion*, V (Spring, 1966), 225–240; "The Pharisaic Revolution," *Perspectives in Jewish Learning*, II (1966), 25–26; "Prolegomenon" to *Judaism and Christianity*, ed. Oesterly and Rosenthal Loewe (New York: Ktav, 1969), pp. XI–LXX; "Ben Sira and the Non-Existence of the Synagogue," *In the Time of Harvest*, ed. D. J. Silver (New York: Macmillan, 1963), pp. 321–354; "Defining the Pharisees," *Hebrew Union College Annual*, XL–XLI (1969–70), 205–49; "Pharisaism and the Crisis of the Individual in the Greco-Roman World," *Jewish Quarterly Review*, LXI (July 1970), 27–53. For prevailing scholarly viewpoints, see A. Michel and I. Le Moyne, "Pharisiens," Supplément au *Dictionnaire de la Bible* (Paris, 1965), Fasciules 39–40, pp. 1022–1115; L. Finkelstein, *The Pharisees*, Third Edition (Philadelphia: Jewish Publication Society of America, 1962); and especially S. Zeitlin, "Ha-Zedukkim ve-ha-Perushim," *Horeb*, III (1936), 56–92, and his *Rise and Fall of the Judean State* (Philadelphia: Jewish Publication Society of America, 1962–1967), passim.

Time, History, and Individual Salvation

This good news of personal salvation, of eternal life, of resurrection transmuted the concept of the peoplehood of Israel and the relationship of this people to both God and the Holy Land. Israel was now conceived of as the brotherhood of the true believers in the gospel of the Father God, the twofold Law, and the promise of eternal life and resurrection. The divine promises were transferred from the nation and the Land to the individual. Salvation depended on adherence to the system of the twofold Law and not on birth. It was therefore available to all individuals, Jew and Gentile. It was operative both inside the Land and outside it, whether the Temple functioned or not, whether the people as a whole took advantage of it or not. To be born an Israelite was an advantage for it gave immediate access to the system of salvation. But it was neither enough nor absolutely essential. An Israelite of the flesh who denied the authority of the twofold Law—and there were many such, as the existence of the Sadducees makes evident—was doomed to eternal punishment, whereas a proselyte who joined himself to Israel was assured life eternal and resurrection.[2] By transferring the rewards and punishments to the world to come and by shifting the focus of salvation from the people and the Land to the individual, the Soferim-Pharisees stripped time of its directional thrust. History was not moving anywhere. Time present, time forward, time prior were indistinguishable in structure and in quality so long as salvation was attainable. One was no closer to eternal life or resurrection *now* than had been an Abraham or a Moses *then*. God was no more the Father *now* than he had been the Father *then*. The individual soul had been as precious *then* as it was *now*.

This timeless quality is beautifully rendered by Josephus, a follower of the Pharisees, in his depiction of the binding of Isaac:

[2]Cf. Josephus, an avowed Pharisee (*Vita* 7–12), on the centrality of eternal life and resurrection in the Pharisaic belief system; *War* II: 163–165b, III: 371–376; *Antiquities* XVIII:14. Cf. also *Sanhedrin* X:1–6, where all of Israel are assured of a share in the world to come, except those who lose it one way or another.

> But when the altar had been prepared and he had cleft the wood upon it and all was ready, he said to his son: "My child, myriad were the prayers in which I besought God for thy birth, and when thou camest into the world, no pains were there that I did not lavish on thine upbringing, no thought had I of higher happiness than to see thee grown to man's estate and to leave thee at my death heir to my dominion. But since it was by God's will that I became thy sire and now again as it pleases him I am resigning thee, bear thou this consecration valiantly; for it is to God I yield thee, to God who now claims from us this homage in return for the gracious favor he has shown me as my supporter and ally.
>
> "Aye, since thou wast born [out of the course of nature, so] quit thou now this life not by the common road *but sped* by thine own father on thy way to God, the Father of all, through the rites of sacrifice. He, I ween, accounts it not meet for thee to depart this life by sickness or war or by any of the calamities that commonly befall mankind, *but amid prayers and sacrificial ceremonies would receive thy soul and keep it near to himself;* and for me thou shalt be a protector and a stay of my old age—to which end above all I nurtured thee—by giving me God instead of thyself."
>
> The son of such a father could not but be brave-hearted, and Isaac received these words with joy.[3]

This is a striking and paradoxical depiction. Josephus, a devotee of the twofold Law and its system of salvation *and* a sophisticated historian who took Thucydides for his model, does not adhere to the literal account in Genesis. He does not simply take liberties with the text but fashions an account out of some other source, a source that was deemed by him more authoritative and binding than the literal rendering. Since this deviation pertains to the belief in the immortal soul and its *immediate* access at death to God the Father, this source must have been an oral teaching that took precedence over the literal meaning of the text. Josephus must have

[3]Josephus, *Antiquities* I:228–232, tr. H. St. J. Thackeray (Loeb Edition; Cambridge: Harvard University Press, 1930), IV, 113–115.

drawn upon the nonwritten lore of the teachers of the twofold Law, a lore that is generically referred to as *Aggadah*, a term not even found in the Bible. Thus Josephus gave preference to an aggadic fact over a biblical fact, even though biblical fact was a written text, antedating the emergence of the twofold Law and a text that was believed by Josephus *and* the teachers of the *Aggadah* as having been dictated by God himself.

By this act of transference, Josephus shatters the biblical demarcations separating structures and ideas in time. Whereas the Pentateuch never blurs the differentiation between the period of the Patriarchs and that of Moses, Josephus treats Abraham and Moses as though they were both sophisticated philosophers and urbane statesmen. He casts the spiritual heroes of Israel's past in the same mold, as though time, place, and structure were largely irrelevant. History is thus nothing other than a record of event jostling event and is headed nowhere. The individual, caught in the mesh of terrestrial happenings, should shape his life by adherence to the twofold Law and should take for his models the great spiritual leaders of Israel who had never deviated from virtue, goodness, and righteousness, despite the lure and pressure of historical circumstances. The temporal world was thus the realm where otherworldly salvation was earned.

The rejection of historical direction was so central to the teaching of the new Soferim-Pharisees that they never chronicled any history at all, not even their own. There is no connected historical narrative to be found in the whole complex of the Oral Law or lore. There is no biography, only item-like paradigms. There is no Soferic-Pharisaic chronicle of the Hasmonean revolt, no sustained narrative of the split between John Hyrcanus and the Pharisees and the subsequent civil war during the reign of Alexander Janneus; no historical account of the evolution of the twofold Law, its teachers, and institutions; no setting down of the events leading to the revolt against Rome and the destruction of the Second Temple. The gospel of the twofold Law, eternal life, and resurrection reduced terrestrial history to irrelevance.

The shift in time perspective had other profound consequences. The entire corpus of Holy Scriptures was now looked upon as expressing the divine will. Although the Pentateuch was still accorded a certain kind of primacy, it was not the only source of

God's revelation. The historical books, the Prophets, and the canonical Hagiographa—all were repositories of God's Word. As such, they could not be in contradiction with one another. Neither Moses, nor Elijah, nor the Psalmist could have disregarded the triadic structure: (1) Father God, (2) twofold Law, (3) eternal life and resurrection for the individual. Every verse was believed either to presuppose this structure or to bear witness to it. Holy Scriptures thus could be drawn upon freely to confirm it, to amplify it, and to enrich it, but never to challenge it. When David, for example, composed the Psalms, the Law that he praised was the twofold Law, the God that he addressed was the Heavenly Father, the hope that sustained him was the world to come and the resurrection.

The assumption that the triadic structure was the leitmotiv of revelation encouraged the exploration of biblical writ for appropriate verses. The interest was no longer centered on the book but on the sentence. What was needed was scriptural proof to clarify a situation, illumine a teaching, underwrite a law, inspire an act. The larger context was irrelevant; it could not inhibit the usage of a verse for salvationary ends. Indeed, what was far more crucial than context was the combining of verses, drawn from different biblical books, to drive home the identical lesson. The fact that a verse in the Pentateuch was reinforced by a verse from the Prophets and confirmed by a verse from the Psalms was the most powerful proof that one could bring for the essential unity and timeless quality of the revelation.

The reawakening of dormant Scriptures thus went hand and hand with its subordination to the triadic structure. Just as the Aaronides had tolerated no challenge to Pentateuchal absolutism and hierocratic hegemony, so the new class of Soferim-Pharisees revived the historical, prophetic, and hagiographic writings to underwrite their authority, not to undercut it. For them, Scripture was a confirmation of, not a challenge to, the twofold Law system of salvation for the individual.

This system needed no messianic concept. So long as the road to salvation was not blocked by insuperable obstacles in this world, all that was necessary was the twofold Law and the firm belief that adherence to it would yield salvation. At death, the soul ascended to

God the Father and there awaited the resurrection, the time and nature of which was left vague and undetermined. To attain this salvation, one needed neither Land nor Temple, nor even the totality of Israel. All that was necessary was the twofold Law, internalized in the conscience of the individual, and the faith that the Heavenly Father would reward one's loyalty with immortality.

Josephus in *Against Apion* expresses this system of belief simply and eloquently:

> For those . . . who live in accordance with our laws the prize is not silver or gold, no crown of wild olive or of parsley with any such public mark of distinction. No; each individual, relying on the witness of his own conscience and the lawgiver's prophecy, confirmed by the sure testimony of God, is firmly persuaded that to those who observe the laws and if they must need die for them willingly meet death, God has granted a renewed existence and in the revolution of the ages the gift of a better life.[4]

Pharisaic Silence Concerning the Messiah

The Scribes-Pharisees never emphasized the messianic concept prior to the destruction of the Temple in the year 70—though there were many occasions that lent themselves admirably to such a doctrine, such as the following:

1. The Hasmonean revolt. Although it was during the Hasmonean revolt that the new scholar class of Soferim-Pharisees came into existence and took charge of the Law, they did not call for the restoration of the Davidic kingdom. Instead, they invested Simon the Hasmonean with the high priesthood—an act in direct violation of Pentateuchal command, which invested Phineas and his descendants with the high priesthood forever (Numbers 25:10–12) and with the ethnarchy.

[4]Josephus, *Against Apion* II: 217b–218, tr. H. St. J. Thackeray (Loeb Edition; Cambridge: Harvard University Press, 1926), I, 351.

2. The split between John Hyrcanus and the Pharisees and the subsequent civil war during the reign of Alexander Janneus. Throughout these bitter years, the Scribes-Pharisees had a single purpose: the restoration of the twofold Law. When this was agreed to by Salome Alexandra, the Scribes-Pharisees were perfectly willing to acknowledge her as queen. They did not disqualify the Hasmonean monarchy because it was non-Davidic. They measured it by a simple test: Did it sanction the operation of the twofold Law, and did it acknowledge the right of the Scribal-Pharisaic leaders to teach it?

3. The reign of Herod. Not only did the Scribes-Pharisees not challenge Herod but their leader Sameias was active in urging the people to open the gates of Jerusalem to him and to acknowledge him as sovereign.

4. The rule of Rome. The Scribes-Pharisees refused to condemn the taking of the census by Quirinius. They declared the issue to be out of religious bounds, even though it meant acquiescing in the levying of the Roman tribute. So principled was this Pharisaic doctrine on the status of the state that when Judas of Galilee insisted that the census should be resisted and the tribute go unpaid, he and his followers were viewed by the Scribes-Pharisees as the founders of a Fourth Philosophy, even though on all other issues Judas and his followers adhered to the teachings of the Scribes-Pharisees.[5]

5. The revolt against Rome. Although at first opposed to the revolt, the Scribal-Pharisaic leadership reluctantly supported it once it had gained irrepressible momentum.[6] Yet at no time during the revolt did Simeon son of Gamalie[7] or Johanan ben Zakkai look to a Messiah to deliver the people. In fact, the latter was far more concerned with getting out of besieged Jerusalem than with messianic hopes.[8]

[5]Cf. *Antiquities* XVIII:1–10, 23–25; *War* II:117–118.

[6]Cf. *Vita* 20–23.

[7]Cf. *War* IV:158–161.

[8]One should also note the fact that nowhere in Agrippa's plea to the people to desist from rebellion does he deal with the messianic hope as one of the illusions held by the people. He merely stresses that God will not come to their aid (*War* II:391–394).

The Scribes-Pharisees thus took no advantage of recurrent opportunities to vivify the messianic concept. It therefore could not have been essential to their system. Indeed, it was in most respects a hazardous and threatening notion. The biblical record was more an indictment of the Davidic dynasty than a model for imitation. Furthermore, the concrete experiences of the Scribes-Pharisees with the Hasmonean, Herodean, and Roman sovereigns revealed only too clearly the dangers inherent in any exploitation of ambiguous and obscure prophecies to sanctify any kind of monarchy, Davidic or otherwise. The biblical verses did not control the Scribes-Pharisees, but the Scribes-Pharisees did control the application of these verses to contemporary situations. The greatest deterrence, however, was the certain knowledge that a Messiah would be most reluctant to subordinate himself to Scribal-Pharisaic authority.

Pseudepigrapha, New Prophecy, and Jesus

Although the turbulent times may not have stirred messianic hopes in the Scribes-Pharisees, they did sow such expectations in others. Indeed, in response to the crisis of confidence in Aaronidism, the very crisis that had given birth to the revolutionary class of Scribes-Pharisees, some unknown writer had looked for some kind of biblical solution. Cut off from access to direct prophecy, he sought to convey God's message for these troublesome times by putting it into the mouth of a prophetlike figure, Daniel. He believed that God would save those who, suffering martyrdom if necessary, remained steadfast to the Law; he was certain that the righteous dead would be resurrected, even as the wicked would suffer eternal humiliation (Daniel 12:1–3).

The problem, as we have seen, was not solved in this way. The Hellenistic threat and the collapse of Aaronide leadership were parried by the Hasmoneon revolt and the Pharisaic revolution. The Book of Daniel was taken at its face value and was believed by the Scribes-Pharisees themselves to have been written in the Babylonian Exile, as claimed. It thus was included among inspired Scripture, and Daniel's predictions were taken neither more nor less seriously than those of Isaiah, Jeremiah, or Ezekiel.

The pseudepigraphic tactic was not, however, discarded. It was turned to again and again, especially as dissatisfaction with the Pharisaic teaching on the state sought some means of overt expression. The Scribes-Pharisees more and more affirmed that the state was of relevant religious concern *only* when the state blocked the road to salvation. So long, however, as the state did not interfere with the teaching and the observance of the twofold Law, it was to be considered as sanctioned by God. This teaching seems to have matured when Sameias, the Pharisaic leader, urged the people to open the gates of Jerusalem to Herod.[9] It was reenforced when the Pharisees refused to oppose the census taken by Quirinius.[10]

This doctrine did not sit well with those Jews who had a deep attachment to independence and strong belief that God must be as concerned with the terrestrial fate of his people, his city, and his Land as with the salvation of the individual. Their dissatisfaction with the Pharisaic teachings on the state was intensified as the harsh policies of the Roman procurators condemned large numbers of Jews to poverty and deprivation. It is not surprising, therefore, that many longed for the God who had actively intervened for Israel in biblical days. Why should he who performed miracles for Israel in the past not perform miracles now as well? Seeking to convince others that God would once again intervene directly, visionaries turned to the pseudepigraphical mode. By doing so, they challenged the Pharisees with prophecy. God was not indifferent to the terrestrial status of Israel. Such a confrontation did not, however, necessarily carry with it a rejection of the Pharisaic belief in eternal life and resurrection for the individual.

But the pseudepigraphous mode was not the only resource open to those yearning for God's breakthrough into history. Prophecy could come alive again through a charismatic Teacher proclaiming that the kingdom of God was at hand; that the world of corruption was about to be swept away; that a Savior to redeem Israel was at hand, the Son of man was about to usher in the day of judgment.

[9]*Antiquities* XV:1–4.
[10]*Antiquities* XVIII:1–10, 23.

Such good news could be preached directly by a living prophet, by a living Son of man, by a living Messiah, who could justify his claims by giving concrete meaning to highly ambiguous predictions of the prophets.[11] The Pharisees could thus be confuted by their own teaching that all of Scripture was the Word of God; that this Word was not trapped in the context of a book; that God's revelation had been both immutable and timeless. He could confront the Scribes-Pharisees with verses wherein Yahweh had promised to David an eternal kingdom and had proclaimed an end of days. He could call upon the grand prophets who had envisioned a Zion restored to peace, serenity, and sovereignty and who had foreseen God's forceful reentry into Israel's history. And when confronted, the Pharisees would be compelled to counter with a messianic concept of their own, a concept that would preserve the prophecies yet offset their application to contemporary situations and to contemporary individuals.

The Pharisaic concept of the Messiah was thus originally defensive. It was more concerned with exposing would-be messiahs than with finding one.

For these ends, there were biblical texts that were most helpful. They could argue that a Messiah is indeed promised in Scripture, but he would have to be able to prove that he was of direct Davidic descent; perform signs equaling those of the prophets of yore; follow the public return of Elijah; be a champion of the twofold Law, a venerator of the Scribes-Pharisees, a teacher of vintage, not newly pressed, doctrine. The bona fides of the Messiah would have to be verified by the authoritative spokesmen for the twofold Law, the Scribes-Pharisees, and by them alone. A self-proclaimed messiah was ipso facto a false messiah.

Such was the stock of messianic thought current among the Scribal-Pharisaic leadership when Jesus began his ministry—clearly no rich lode of esoteric doctrine but an arsenal of confutations. It was meager to begin with and became enlarged only to the degree that new ideological weapons were fashioned to blunt the power of new claims. The Scribes-Pharisees are thus accurately de-

[11] *War* II:258–265; *Antiquities* XVIII:116–119; XX:98–99.

picted in the Gospels as devising stumbling blocks to Jesus' efforts to gain a hearing.

The cross normally was the end of the road, the proof positive that the would-be messiah had been a fraud. For Jesus and his disciples, the crucifixion should have been equally definitive. His bona fides had been exposed as fraudulent. Once again the Scribes-Pharisees had been confirmed. The kingdom of God had not been ushered in for all to see. Jesus crucified should have been a mockery, not a vindication.

Yet we know, Jews no less than Christians, that the cross was the beginning, not the end. It was the birth of a viable and vital messianic idea, an idea proclaimed by Jews, for Jews, and out of the stuff of regnant Judaism. What gave life to the crucified Messiah was the Pharisaic belief in the resurrection of the dead. Agonizing, despairing, and stunned, the grief-stricken disciples clutched at the core hope of the Pharisaic system: the belief that the Heavenly Father would reward the righteous with eternal life and resurrection. Just as Abraham had had faith when binding Isaac that he was dispatching his beloved son to God the Father, so every true believer in the twofold Law had faith that all who were righteous would be so rewarded. It dawned on them that the proof of Jesus' claim to be Christ was his resurrection. The disciples had been misled. The Messiah had not proved himself while alive but by the awesome fact of resurrection. Only the stubborn could deny such a sign. Jesus had been crucified; he had risen. Just as the disciples had been witness to the first fact, they were now also witness to the second. For them, to deny that they had seen him resurrected was as inconceivable as to deny that he had been crucified.

Here now was a problem for the Scribes-Pharisees that had not been anticipated. The unusual had occurred. A messianic claimant had not died on the cross. His disciples were testifying that Jesus had risen from the dead. The Pharisaic belief in the resurrection was being called upon to confirm Jesus' claim to be the Messiah. The Pharisees could not deny the possibility of resurrection. They proclaimed that the resurrection was to be anticipated as an empirically verifiable phenomenon. It was not as easy for them to disprove the Second Coming as it had been to disprove the First.

Paul—Pharisee and Christian

Paul attests to the turmoil of a Pharisee who wrestled with the fact of Jesus' resurrection. By his own testimony (Philippians 3:6), Paul had been a Pharisee, and a precocious one at that. He had prided himself on his commitment to the *paradosis*, the Oral Law. He could boast that his righteousness under the Law had been blameless. He had not known the living Jesus. It was the claim that Jesus had been resurrected that had stirred him to zealous persecution of the church. From the outset the only Christ Paul had known had been the risen one. This was the Christ that had aroused his fury. As a Pharisee, he did not confront a living claimant but a resurrected one.

And a frenzied Pharisee Paul was. "For you have heard of my former life in Judaism," he reminds the Galatians, "how I persecuted the church of God violently and tried to destroy it" (Galatians 1:13). And just as his hostility expressed in the Epistle to the Philippians (3:6) was tightly linked to his commitment to the twofold Law, so his confession of hounding the church in Galatians goes hand in hand with his precocious loyalty to Pharisaic Judaism: "And I advanced in Judaism beyond many of my own age among my people, so extremely zealous was I for the traditions [the *paradosis*, i.e., the Oral Law] of my Fathers" (Galatians 1:14).

Why this persecuting zeal? Was it not because Paul's personal salvation was at stake? The Pharisees proclaimed the gospel of God the Father. They taught the twofold Law as his revelation. They promised eternal life and resurrection to the faithful and the obedient. Resurrection was the reward for loyalty to Pharisaism. No one could be resurrected who had been disloyal. Yet the disciples of Jesus preached Jesus the resurrected Christ, the very Jesus who had, in his lifetime, set himself up as a law unto himself. He had challenged the Pharisees and defied them. He had refused to permit the Pharisees to evaluate his messianic bona fides. He had stubbornly persisted in putting forth his claims and had ended up on the cross. Now his disciples were proclaiming that this challenger of Pharisaic authority had risen from the dead. This could not be! Resurrection was the reward for obedience, not rebellion. This pernicious, false, and dangerous teaching must be rooted out! As a zealous champion of the twofold Law, Paul must take the lead in exposing this fraudulent gospel.

But doubt lurked behind Paul's righteous determination. What if Jesus had risen? What if his resurrection were a fact? What if the proof of Christ *was* the resurrection?

This doubt gnawed at him and gave him no rest. The more he persecuted, the more fragile became his certainty; the more he hounded, the more he doubted. Surging from the deepest recesses of his being, powerful passions threatened to break through the dikes of the internalized Law. The pressure of sinful impulses began to batter away at the carefully constructed defenses, barring them from consciousness. He began to perceive another law at war with the law of his mind, making him captive to the law of sin dwelling in his senses. And suddenly there came a moment of wretched doubt; the dikes would no longer hold; the internal defenses were overwhelmed; and Paul collapsed into Christ and was revived.

Jesus, Paul now knew, had risen from the dead. He was the Christ. He was the Son of God. He sat at his Father's side. It was now all so clear. The Law does not lead to salvation. It is not the road to eternal life and resurrection. It is not the way to overcome the power of sin. The Law is a delusion. It hides the fact that behind the Law sin lurks. The Law does not vanquish sin. It merely holds it off, blocks its overt activity, screens it from consciousness, serves as a defense. But the power of sin is not extinguished by it. It persists through the very commandments themselves. Every "Thou shalt not" is a provocation—stirring sin to activity and awareness of its power in the impulses and senses of man. Unaided, man cannot master the power of sin. Law is a defense, not a solution. God the Father, aware of man's helplessness, had sent his Son as an act of grace to deliver him from the power of sin and death. Christ had come to redeem man from sin, not Roman rule. Jesus had come to Israel with the gospel of eternal life and resurrection, the free and gracious gift of God the Father. Eternal life and resurrection were through Christ and not, as the Pharisees taught, the reward for obedience to the twofold Law (cf. Epistle to the Romans, especially chapter 7).

Paul's solution was profound. His gospel of Christ as the Redeemer from sin freed the messianic idea from the shackles of time and space. Although Paul anticipated that Jesus would shortly return and although there are apocalyptic patches in his gospel, his core teaching was not dependent on Christ's imminent return. The redemptive power of Christ was continuously active in every individual who had faith in him. One did not have to wait for Christ to return because Christ had not really gone away. He was inside the believing individual no less than he was outside. He could be internalized so securely that one lived in Christ because Christ lived in him. Secure in Christ's internalized presence, the individual was released from the fetters of externality. Space and time lost their reality to Reality itself. Slave or freeman, man or woman, Greek or Jew, the individual was threatened by sin *now* and Christ was there to help him *now*.

Paradoxically, however, Paul's Christ is structurally congruent with the Pharisaic system of the twofold Law. Each was believed by its devotees to be the creation of God the Father. Each promises to deliver from sin and each offers eternal life and resurrection for the believing individual. Each preaches that Reality is within, not without. Each denies to *externality* the power to refute the certainties of an *internalized* faith. And each acknowledges that the Messiah will come—or come again—but until that unknown and perhaps unknowable day, salvation is at hand: for the Pharisees in the twofold Law, for Paul in the ever-redeeming Christ.

Messiah in Christianity and Judaism

I have concentrated on Paul because the development of Christianity followed the road mapped by him more so than that which was opened up by the Jewish disciples of Jesus who had known and loved the living Jesus. Although they too preached the risen Christ, they failed to grasp the elemental power of Christ as the unique Redeemer from sin and the substitute for the Law. They were too attached to the Jesus who had lived, healed, and preached for Jews, to Jews, and about Jews. They were too caught up in the terrestrial messianic goals of the preresurrected Jesus to abandon them completely after he had risen. They were too dependent on his coming back again to accomplish what he had left undone for Israel in his lifetime. Paul's stand on the status of the Law was for them too ambivalent. They were frightened by Paul's devastating denunciation of the Law as the agent provocateur of sin, and they could not proclaim that his was *the* essential teaching of the cross. The non-Pauline Gospels were important, but not as potent as the Gospel of Paul. The ultimate collapse of the Law within the Christian church—despite Matthew—and the ultimate peopling of the church with Gentiles—not Jews—would seem to leave little doubt that Paul's gospel was triumphant.

The messianic idea of Jesus and Paul was nonetheless a creation of Judaism. Jesus had lived and taught as a Jew, while Paul had agonized over the reality of the resurrection as a zealous follower of the twofold Law. What is more, Paul sought to convince himself and others that Holy Scriptures, the very source of the Law, had foretold Christ's coming to redeem Israel from its helplessness and provocation to sin. Paul's entire plea that faith, not acts of the Law, is the true righteousness is dependent on Scripture as God's revelation (Romans 3–4). So, too, the Four Gospels. All rest their claims for Jesus as the Christ, both before and after the resurrection, on biblical writ as the Word of God.

There is a point in time, however, when the Christian concept of the Messiah ceases to be Jewish. Once the Law is abandoned and once the church is predominantly gentile, Messiah for the Christians becomes the central core of their faith; whereas for Jews, he continues to remain, as he had earlier, an open and ambivalent possibility.

The success of Christianity, however, did alter the concept significantly for Judaism. The teachers of the twofold Law could not ignore the challenge posed by Scriptures. They were therefore compelled to take the idea more seriously than they had done before, if only to dilute the appeal of the Jewish Christians. The Messiah, they affirmed, would indeed come. He would deliver the people from their external enemies. He would restore the Temple. He would return the exiles to the land. He would be a son of David. He would fulfill any number of prophetic predictions. He might even perform miracles, usher in the day of judgment, arouse the dead from their graves. Indeed, the real Messiah would do everything that a real Messiah is meant by God to do. What fantasy could not imagine, reality would make good.

He would some day come. In fact, the promise was gradually translated into a dogma, inserted in the daily prayers, and ultimately set down by Maimonides as an article of faith. But faith in a promise is one thing; fulfillment is something quite other. The pressure for a messianic solution came whenever the pain and degradation in the external world bordered on the unendurable. Tempest-tossed, following on the destruction of the Temple in the year 70, the Jews played out most of their subsequent history in the Diaspora. They clung to their faith as minority groupings within larger and far more powerful societies. They were sometimes treated benignly, sometimes roughly. Now they were granted the right of settlement, now deprived of it. They were not only dispersed far from the Holy Land, but they periodically underwent exile from lands they had come to love and neighbors whom they had come to cherish. Pogroms followed privileges, impoverishment always licked at the heels of prosperity. And in Christian countries, they were never allowed to forget that for the majority, Christ, the son of David, had already come for the Israel of the spirit that had recognized him.

The tides of history were understood neither by Jews, Christians, nor Muslims. The Jews did not know why they themselves were tossed about. They did not know why the seas were sometimes rough, sometimes calm, sometimes washing them to shore, sometimes dashing them on the rocks, sometimes setting them adrift with no star to guide them. Their only compass was the belief that God had chosen them and had made known his revelation in the twofold Law. When despairing, they could comfort themselves with the faith that life eternal awaited their souls and resurrection their bodies. The world might be going nowhere and history might be driftless, but the soul would soar to their Father in heaven and there, in the midst of adoring angels, it would find repose.

But man, being the creature he is, has rarely been content with the promise of eternal life alone. He longs to have this life as well. He wishes that God would grant him both. He sees no reason why it cannot be. Abraham was promised a this-worldly land. Moses led his people to the edge of a terrestrial land flowing with milk and honey. God over and over again had assured his people that if they would obey him, their this-worldly granaries would be full and their harvests abundant. The prophets had predicted a joyous, earthly Zion for the scattered Israel of Yahweh. Prodded by cataclysmic events and impatient with the cruel bludgeonings of history, individuals frequently read the signs of the times as evidence that the Messiah was at hand. The dormant texts once again would spring to life. God's meaning once again would be writ clear. The time was fulfilled, the kingdom of God was at hand, the Messiah had come.

With the possible exceptions of Bar Kochba and Sabbetai Zevi, all such readings were discounted, refuted, and mocked by the scholar class in authority, who read the signs and their meanings quite differently. When the pretender failed to come through, when he ultimately suffered death, it was clear that the texts had indeed been misread and God's will, with respect to the Messiah, still remained inscrutable. And the people would once again consign their faith in the Messiah to dreamlike fantasies, concentrate on the observance of the Law, and hope for the world to come that did not have to wait for the coming of the Messiah.

The messianic idea thus could neither be abandoned nor embraced so long as Judaism was rooted in the belief in the divine revelation of Scriptures and in the teachings of the twofold Law. The rootage determined the branches and their fruit.

Modern Notions

With the emergence of the modern Western world, the authoritative grip of scriptural and twofold Law relaxed. A liberal form of Judaism, which transmuted the messianic idea, made its appearance in nineteenth-century Germany. No longer committed to literal revelation and freed from the bind of the twofold Law system of salvation, spokesmen for this liberal movement gave the messianic a historical and directional meaning. Judaism, so they claimed, taught the coming of a Messianic Age through the processes of historical evolution and development. Jews were looking to an age of human fulfillment, not to the coming of an individual. God's kingdom would be ushered in by man's efforts to construct an ideal world. The prophets, so they noted, had had such a vision of the direction of history, a vision that had been mangled and distorted by the proof-texting technique in the interests of otherworldly salvation and of a personal Messiah.

This notion of a Messianic Age as the outcome of history proved to be very appealing, for it enabled Jews to westernize without abandoning Judaism. If Judaism was neither literal revelation nor binding law but an evolutionary and developmental process, the forms and concepts of earlier modes were instructive and inspirational but not mandatory.

Western Judaism effected one transmutation, Zionism another. At the turn of the century, the overwhelming majority of Jews lived in Eastern Europe. Unlike their Western coreligionists, they had scant hope for emancipation. Subjected to harsh and discriminatory legislation, expelled from most of Russia, and hemmed into a narrow Pale of Settlement, the Jews of Russia and Poland desperately sought a way out of their misery and humiliation. Jewish intellectuals were too westernized to settle for the traditional answers and too bruised to expect emancipation from the tzarist regime.

Excited by the nationalist ideologies intoxicating the intellectual elites throughout all of Europe—but most especially in the multinational, disintegrating empires of Austria-Hungary, Turkey, and Russia—and stirred by the unique achievement of the Jewish people—a historical accomplishment unequaled by any other—gifted and sensitive leaders such as Herzl, Pinsker, and others championed the idea of Jewish nationalism. Committed to the national spirit as the élan vital of the Jewish people and assigning to Judaism only a secondary role, these leaders saw shimmering through the religious notion of the Messiah a more elemental national consciousness. The messianic idea had kept the nation alive by focusing the hope of the scattered people on a restoration to their land and their polity. What had preserved the Jews through the centuries had been neither the Law nor the promise of eternal life and resurrection but an irrepressible longing to go home again. Paradoxically, those Jews most committed to the belief that God would send his Messiah were, and still are, the most antagonistic to the national idea.

The Jews of today thus reveal the full spectrum of the historical vicissitudes of the messianic idea. There are Orthodox Jews who believe in eternal life, the resurrection, and the coming of the Messiah as articles of faith. There are Conservative Jews with diverse opinions. There are Reform Jews who look to a Messianic Age. There are nationalist Jews who see the rebirth of Israel as the fulfillment of the messianic idea in the establishment of a secular, self-governing, and secure state. And there are Jews who have never given the matter much thought.

If, then, we turn to the Christian experience, we see how similar it has been to the Jewish experience. Once the church had resigned itself to the fact that Jesus would not soon return, it concentrated on the Christ within and the assurances that his presence gave the true believer that he could overcome sin and gain for himself eternal life and resurrection. The belief in the Second Coming was never abandoned, but the church, no more than the synagogue, was careless about the bona fides of would-be Christs. The church, like the synagogue, had to contend with an external world that was as cruel as it was bewildering. Suffering Christians, like suffering Jews, wished that they could have the best of both worlds—this world and the world to come. For many, Christ within was not sufficient to still the pain, allay the hunger, erase the misery, and restore the shattered self-esteem. When hunger stalked the land, and war ravaged the fields, and plague snatched off the young and not so young, even pious Christians could not but hear the Second Coming in the resounding hoofs of the horses of the apocalypse dinning in their ears. Yet the church, like the synagogue, was wary of even the clearest signs and omens, and it sought to expose the Antichrists who taunted the faithful with devilish signs. In each instance, the empirical proof was for the church, as for the synagogue, determinative. The Pharisees asked Jesus for a sign; they looked for evidence that Elijah had come; they wanted a genealogy that could be checked; and above all, they wanted *their* authority to determine who was the Messiah to be acknowledged. The history of the church shows that its leaders were no less circumspect.

For Jews, however devout, Messiah will never come. They will no more be able to distinguish him from a pretender than their forefathers could distinguish Jesus from other claimants. For Christians, the Messiah has indeed come, but it is questionable whether his Second Coming would be any more easily recognized by Christians than by the Scribes-Pharisees of yore. But perhaps in some mysterious way this is God's teaching about the Christ. Whether it be the internalized twofold Law, the internalized Christ, or the internalized principle of God's governance of the universe and of man, God's *eternal* kingdom is within, an *internal* kingdom.